PILGRIMAGE TO THE REBIRTH

CHARLES O. GINGERICH

PILGRIMAGE TO THE REBIRTH

Erlo van Waveren

SAMUEL WEISER INC., New York

Unity School Library
Unity Village, MO 64065

© 1978 BY ERLO VAN WAVEREN

All rights reserved. No part of this publication may be reproduced or transmitted in any form or by any means, electronic or mechanical, including photocopy, recording, or any information storage and retrieval system, without permission in writing from the publisher.

ISBN 0-87728-420-2

Printed in the U.S.A.
Set, printed and bound by
The Book Press, Brattleboro, Vt.

THIS TALE OF MY SPIRIT IS DEDICATED

TO MY MUCH LOVED AND LOVELY WIFE

Ann.

Her courage and unfailing search for truth, her support of the timeless memories of my spirit, and her sweet curiosity gave my Self the opportunity to write this tale of my psychic life.

On this page Ann and I want to pay tribute to Carl Gustav Jung. It is Dr. Jung — the august Carl — who has given us the tools to understand more of our psyche, of which we are, to quote him, "so pitifully unaware." We love that man very much, and he often symbolises for us the great Wise Man in our dreams.

ACKNOWLEDGMENTS

Gratefully I have accepted the help of many, but those who follow are very special to me.

THEO. E. YOUNG came several summers in succession to Zürich to help distill out of my unconscious the full story of the Pilgrimage, which I had written in my diary in an almost skeleton form. His great contribution is that he insisted on my own style and forced me into further clarifications.

In Zürich, I received much encouragement from my Jungian friends ANIELLA JAFFE and CORNELIA BRUNNER as well as the Drs. YECHESKEL and RIWKAH KLUGER from Haifa.

In Oxford, Dr. MARGARET WILEY MARSHALL was very helpful with some early editing. She and her late husband, Dr. RODERICK MARSHALL, have been very supportive of my myth.

OLIVIER BERNIER was of great help with his typing and keen observations. ANDOR BRAUN, who undertook the design and shepherded this book through the presses had a scrutinizing eye for "le mot juste", for which I am most grateful.

It seems so appropriate that the owners of an old American priory, TOM and HARRIE SCHLOSS, are responsible for a most thoughtful and generous financial arrangement. Last but not least, it is IRINA PABST, on the board of Wainwright House in Rye, N.Y., who helped to smooth the way so that this outstanding institution of the humanities and Jungian thought could be the support behind this publication.

To all my friends again my heartfelt thanks.

FOREWORD

THOUGH my husband and I have accepted the fact that there are mysteries in life that cannot be explained, but must just be accepted, we were still unprepared for the revelations in this book. They were received at times with incredulity and awe, but never denied. For many years, however, we kept them to ourselves, never expecting to place them before the public eye. But life often brings about an unexpected demand.

Reincarnation is an important aspect of this book. We had accepted reincarnation as a probability, but had never liked loose and easy talk about past lives, believing always that this present life, fully lived, is the one of importance. Hence we had never attempted to explore our past lives. It was thus with the greatest shock of surprise that we were forced to give our attention to them.

Nor did my husband ever expect to write a book about those lives. However, as he reveals, he was forced to keep a record, and this volume is the result. It is in the form of a myth, his myth, as it were. All of us carry a myth, life's splendid tale lived out in us, whether we know it or not. Since time immemorial, people have spun legends and myths, symbolic tales that hold a truth impossible to express in everyday words. One's own myth is the story of a psychic truth which we are living; sometimes too harsh to take literally, but nevertheless true and laden with meaning. It is the journey of the soul. That journey has meaning not only for the individual, but for others as well.

This book is based upon dreams and visions, both of which have been rather suspect since the Reformation. But in ancient times it was taken for granted that dreams and visions contained important meanings — and again in this century, they seem to be gaining in importance. These meanings have been interpreted by special persons with insight into such phenomena. The medicine man, or shaman, was a well known and deeply revered figure, and still is in certain cultures. It is not just in the Bible that we have records of dreams. In Roman history, there are the well recorded dreams of Scipio, Hannibal and Caesar; in Plato, we have a record of Socrates' dreams. Lincoln's prophetic dream just before his assassination is known in American history. Religious literature is full of the dreams and visions of saints and mystics. Visions, too, have great importance. They appear, in a waking state, often as symbols, and should be interpreted as one would interpret a dream.

There is much talk at the present time about the Aquarian Age. Our earth is constantly moving through the twelve signs of the Zodiac. It takes about two thousand years for the earth to move through each sign, and as we approach the end of the sign of Pisces, we enter the sign of Aquarius: the Aquarian Age. Each sign has its peculiar symbolism, which seems to be reflected in the civilization and religion of that era. For instance, Pisces is the sign of the Fishes, and the fish is important as a Christian symbol. Fish live in the water, and often go in schools. Hence groups were important in the Piscean Age. Organizations flourished.

With the waning of an era, great changes take place, and there is much disruption. The old is receding into the past; the new is not yet stabilized and evident. The old consciousness is becoming the basis for the new. The old concept of Christianity is slipping over the horizon of consciousness, to become the fertilizing factor in the new Age of Aquarius. The symbol of the Aquarian sign is the Waterman, who holds a jar containing the waters of life. An individual consciousness is now required, which forms that container, and we can no longer live unconsciously like a fish.

One change that is already appearing in the world is the prominence of the dark side of life: evil, we call it. In Christianity, the black fish was suppressed as much as possible and only the white fish was accepted. The water jar of Aquarius, however, contains a wholeness that was not present in Pisces. Black and white are both there, intermingled. No longer can the black remain hidden and unredeemed. Both are in life. The consciousness of the individual must provide the resolution. That is the task for the Aquarian Age.

The casual reader who picks up this volume may find it totally irrelevant to the realities of life today, especially if he tries to approach life on a completely rational basis. But another type of reader, searching for something out of the ordinary trend of thought, with a mind open to the irrational side of life, will find it both revealing and illuminating.

Ann van Waveren

PREFACE

THIS BOOK is written out of the pain of the inner man. I belong to those who have been forced to travel a road of self-awareness and, in doing so, I have had to become better acquainted with the Self, that composite nucleus which holds my very essence. Not everybody has to make the journey I have logged here. I offer this tale to those whose need for inner contact has made itself known.

This inner journey is an ancient road. Thousands upon thousands have had to face the realities of the spirit knowingly, but millions upon millions have trod the same road without realizing where they were going or what was happening to them.

The language of this road is always symbolic: the directions are seldom received in direct communication.

My travels through the ages past, my contacts with my inner signposts, my angels, my Christ, the symbols of Aquarius and of the Piscean Age, the divine language of the deep layers of the unconscious, all have come to me through words I often could not comprehend until I became aware that ancestral psychic components were compelling me to write a song — a song of divine and human beings, a song of agony and delight, a song of opposites in which one would balance the other.

My outer life seldom reflected these so-called poetic times. What storms were raging in my inner being! How I had to bend and buckle under those immense unconscious forces! They were unconscious at first; but slowly, as they jousted with my ego, I came to understand their purpose and to realize that this was a symbolic quest.

They told me a story of change, a story of the endless changes of life, a story of death and rebirth. I became aware of the cosmic paths of our sun through the Houses of the Zodiac, and how, with that cosmic rotation, our Sun-God has to go through his evolution in order to experience through man the changes inherent in his own Being.

In this endless round of change, on the wheel of life, I found myself bound — bound tightly to the cosmic changes and the consequent personal changes in my own poor limited mind.

I suffered, I groaned, but relentlessly the great Song of my soul kept pounding its rhythms in the almost incomprehensible language of the symbol.

So here I give you the Song of my soul. I hope it will not be too painful. Perhaps you are my companion on this road; perhaps the story of this symbolic journey through my inner being is just what you need. Then you are not so alone and, for a moment, we will sing a duet, you my reader and I, and then silently we will go each our own way. But you will know that somewhere there is a kindred soul who could, like a scribe, write down God's language, Soul language. And then you may understand what this song of mine is about, in spite of the many mysteries that will remain hidden from both of us.

Be willing to read the well nigh incomprehensible pilgrimage of a wayfarer in the land of his ancestors. I pray that it may bring us into a companionship — even though we may not know each other.

As this book goes out to unknown hands, I reveal my innermost agonies and delights. Guard these precious jewels well and share their worth with those you love, as deep within my heart I love you. I give you this secret, which I have kept hidden even from myself — until today.

A NECESSARY INTRODUCTION

> *"The dream is a little hidden door in the innermost and most secret recesses of the psyche, opening into that cosmic night which was psyche long before there was an ego consciousness and which will remain psyche no matter how far our ego consciousness may extend."*
>
> C. G. Jung

In 1955 I dreamed that the Buddha appeared through a round hole — the Breathing Hole of Eternity —, stepped on the foot of my bed and then onto the floor, where he seated himself in the Lotus position. He communicated the thought that I was to seat myself in his lap and spray my semen in the form of a peacock's tail on his chest.

This dream is the unexpected demand which my wife refers to in her introduction. To me, the Buddha is a world spirit of enfolding and divine consciousness, capable of human existence. The request of that great power has been the driving force behind this revelation of my innermost being. The peacock's tail is found on many ancient tombs as a sign of rebirth.

But it all started in 1945. My wife and I were spending the weekend on the beautiful estate of Meudon on the north shore of Long Island. As

I look back, it seems a long, long time ago. The estate is now Lattingtown Village. Some of our friends and acquaintances presently live facing the greenhouse gardens, another lives in the groom's house, and our oldest friend resides with her family in the butler's cottage by the small pond still there. We have all grown considerably older — and I hope wiser — since then.

I will never forget that weekend. We were staying with our friends in the groom's house, which was charmingly and simply rebuilt. The warm hospitality of our hostess, the long walks on the beach and in the woods thrust us deep in ourselves. On Monday morning, we would go back to the big city. It was in the night from Sunday to Monday that I had the Great Dream which started a new chapter in my life, bringing with it a life full of loneliness and secrecy.

I awoke that Monday morning between three and four with a terrifying shock. I had dreamed that I was on my way to primary school in my home town of Haarlem, in Holland. I was not a young schoolboy in my dream, but my own age, the early forties. The streets were all exactly the way they still are in that old city. At the crossroads just before the block on which my school was located, there appeared out of the sky a great fatherly figure, his head faintly outlining the sturdy contours of my father's skull. I did not see any particular features. However, I knew right away that this was a manifestation of the Godhead, — still, I called him Father Time. His legs never showed — only his immense torso and face. He stretched out his arm, right or left, I don't remember exactly — more likely the left arm — and blessed me, making the sign of the Cross. Automatically, I raised my right arm and blessed him, and while making the sign of the Cross to Him, I noticed that I had in my hand a dishmop, the kind I still use in the kitchen to wash dishes. The next moment, I was transported to the other side of life, and for an infinitesimal time I was in the world of the dead. I felt no pain, but just the same I wept and shrieked out in agony. Again, a sudden shift in my dream brought me back to the street, and, there at the crossroads, invisible hands put me in a blue serge suit, which was rather tight on me and chafed slightly under my arms. I protested to the Heavenly Father that He changed my clothing without asking me if I wanted it changed or if I liked it. There was no answer from Him. Then He blocked the way to my school and pointed towards my right, where the old narrow streets lead to the middle of the town, the marketplace.

I woke up in sheer terror. The power of this visionary dream shook me to the bottom of my soul. I knew that I would die. I had seen the face of God. I had been in His shattering presence. It was of no help to me that the night before I had dreamt of the same street, crowded with people, carrying candles in their hands. They were celebrating a service which, for a short moment, had transported me to the land of the dead.

I got out of bed; though I am in the habit of recording my dreams, it didn't even occur to me to write this one down. Instead, I started to write my last will in the back of my dream book. In large letters I wrote so it could not be overlooked, ever. My life would finish, if not that day then soon after. The shock was such that I didn't even tell the dream to my wife or speak of my apprehension. As Jungian analysts, my wife and I always tell each other our dreams and our notebooks are, to this day, next to our beds.

On the way to New York City I expected a crash. I didn't stop praying during the entire trip of one hour and a half. But nothing happened on that beautiful spring morning. We both saw our clients in the afternoon, and by dinnertime I had enough courage, still being alive, to tell my wife that I needed to speak to her about a startling dream of the early morning.

So after dinner we sat in our little green room, named after the dark green walls the former owner had ingeniously decorated. I started to speak slowly and hesitantly, for the moment I put my attention to the content of my dream I was aware again of an awe in me towards that Heavenly Figure — St. Augustine's experience led him to write about "a spiritual force which the mind was unable to grasp."

All my life I had been forced by circumstances not to follow the academic path. Finances were never the trouble, but emotionally, I was unsuited and too heavily burdened by my complexes to pursue an academic career. Also, my powerful father always wished me to become a merchant and not a doctor like his brother, although that would have been my mother's choice. So when Father Time blocked my way to school, I readily recognized that as a pattern of my life. Professor

Jung, who advised several of my confrères to become doctors, never suggested that road to me. Neither did he ever ask about my studies, which were mostly done in my later teens with private tutors. In my early twenties, I traveled to several countries where there were branches of the family business; hence my stay in America.

But why now this dream? Why call God the Father, Father Time for that question stuck very much in my memory. Why that sedate blue suit, which was binding under my arms? Why those blessings? All these questions were not answered until much later. That night, in the little green room, deeply under the influence of the confrontation, I started to philosophize about my life — the different road I had traveled from that of my mercantile brothers, and the great decision, after my father's death, to leave the family business and to start out for myself. That was a totally fresh and new idea to me, so different from the semi-feudal background in which I had been forced to follow the family tradition.

After a while, I stretched out on the sofa and, traveling further into myself, I began to understand more about my future life. My breathing became deeper and deeper and directed my thought world. I became aware of having a task in life, a destiny all my own, dictated by something within me — the soul, or perhaps the Self, to use a Jungian term for our totality. I found myself telling Ann the purpose of both my present and former life as naturally as if I had been gossiping over a cup of tea. I remember one sentence clearly when, with real humor, my inner voice first bemusedly told my wife, "Well, we could have found perhaps a better one" — and then, addressing itself to me, said, "but you will do."

Because of this voice which spoke from rock bottom, I was firmly convinced that in my former life I had been a teacher of life's values and had returned to continue in that work. I had not solved the message of the dream, but I knew that a greater force in me was now directing my personal life, and that my own ego and personality would have to learn a few things to adjust. I realized that I was on a new, rather constricted, road which at the same time was the continuation of an old one. Then I sat up, punch drunk and still deep within myself.

With the catalytic curiosity of a true wife, Ann asked me naturally and oh, so calmly, "But have you any idea who you were?" And just as calmly "it" spoke right through me and I said "Fénelon." I was stunned, and could have been knocked over with a feather. Ann, not quite remembering his name, asked, "Who is he?" So I looked in the encyclopedia to refresh my memory. While she went to the kitchen to make me a hot drink, I started to read about this French archbishop, a rather controversial figure at the court of Louis XIV. Towards the end of the essay, I became emotionally so upset that I slammed the book shut. Direct memory and a highly charged state of consciousness took over, and I experienced the deep emotions which Fénelon had not been able to assimilate at the beginning of the eighteenth century. I paced the room and, stopping in front of the bookcase, I pointed towards the line of encyclopedias and said: "Before Fénelon, I was Lord Gray, with an *a* or an *e*, and he is hidden in those books too."

After calming down with my warm drink and recovering my everyday senses, I said to my wife: "Well, what this all means, I don't know. I will have to look at my dreams to explain this, and to find out whether it is all an emotional projection and a psychological truth or an actual fact." For eleven years I had been analysed and was analysing myself. Our yearly trips to Zürich before World War II to work with Professor Jung and listen to his private seminars as well as his university lectures, had played an immense role in our lives, and we are still deeply dependent on our dreams to show us the real state of affairs.

So that night I went to bed feeling rather skeptical about my eternal world, reincarnation, and being in the grip of ancient memories. Nevertheless I was undeniably impressed by the power and emotional content of an inner experience so foreign to me. My dreams would have to tell me how to accept this baffling revelation – and they did.

The next morning on awakening I had the confirmation. That night I had dreamt that I was being led first into an oriental chamber. A leather ball was placed on the floor right at the entrance. I gave it a firm kick, very reminiscent of my boyhood soccer days, and the ball hit smack in the middle of a gong, a bull's-eye shot. I can still remember the vibrating sound, sonorous, full and round, as if the entire world should hear it. Then I was brought to the Hall of Justice, situated at right angles to the Oriental section. I entered into an atmosphere of profound truth and integrity, where no law of nature could be trespassed. Several people sat on benches and were listening as my most rational, mercantile, worldly brother tried to sunder his relationship with his newly acquired fiancée.

The judge was seated on a raised paneled platform, listening to my brother, who was trying to get back the diamond he had given his future wife. The judge refused the request. The marriage had to take place. Thus my most rational side had to accept the new link with the unconscious; an alliance had to be made and the stunning revelations of the night before accepted. Then the judge raised his right arm and pointed at nine more diamonds suspended in mid air, representing, with their different sizes and intensities of brilliance, nine former lives with which my most worldly side, as well as my spiritual side, had to get acquainted. With another flash, there appeared the diamond representing my present life. At that I awoke in turmoil.

What a rebellion there was in my twentieth-century, civilized, sophisticated being. In fact, such was my resistance that when, a few weeks later, a dream started to refer to another life of mine, I swung my arms wildly in my sleep and broke through the dream world into my daily consciousness. My only memory was that it was another bishop whose name started with a "W". Several weeks after that I dreamed of a fern with five stalks, representing five bishop's crosiers. They were growing right at the corner of our house in the country. So I was in for it, serious and troublesome times lay ahead of me.

At that time, Cary Baynes, the translator of the English edition of the *I Ching* and her sister, Mrs. Henri Zinno, were the only friends in whom my wife and I dared to confide. We were in deep isolation, even from our own psychological world.

Five years later, in 1950, I spoke with Professor Jung about these surprising developments. In our conversation, he was as open, frank and revelatory as he would ever be with me. Our discussion then was at such an intimate level that the next day he requested Mrs. Jung to speak to me at the Jung Institute and tell me not to talk to anyone about our conversation. In our Western world, Eastern concepts are often sooner accepted when presented in a more or less scientific light. Professor Jung was a past master at that. Whenever he spoke to me about an incarnation, it was referred to as an ancestor; "ancestral components," "psychic ancestors," "ancestral souls" are all expressions which Professor Jung used to express the idea of metamorphosis with which I am dealing in this book.

Through my dreams, I became aware of the ancestral heritage of my present day life. I visited many of the places connected with my psychic components, which was most interesting but trying at times. Curiously enough, those visits integrated my "characters" very much into the Now of my present day, twentieth-century self.

In *Memories, Dreams, Reflections* Professor Jung writes:

"It had been asked by, as it were, my spiritual forefathers in the hope and expectation that they would learn what they had not been able to find out during their time on earth, since the answers first had to be created in the centuries that followed. . . . If question and answer had already been in existence in eternity, had always been there, no effort on my part would have been necessary and it could all have been discovered in any other century. There does seem to be unlimited knowledge present in nature, it is true, but it can be comprehended by consciousness only when the time is ripe for it."

For me that time is now. To paraphrase Paul, who lived nearly 2000 years ago, "the trumpet shall sound, and the dead shall be raised, incorruptible; we shall not die."

It has taken twenty centuries, but now it can be written with conviction that the dead can return incorruptible to the state of consciousness they had in past centuries and continue their psychic awareness now and in future ages. Indeed, time is not.

The manifestation of God as Father Time in the dream is for me a sign that my unconscious wants me to be aware of the changing times in the Godhead. The Piscean Age of Christian endeavor is drawing to its close and is making way for the Age of Aquarius.

December 14, 1968
New York City
11:30 P.M.

NEVER, NEVER in my life had I thought I would write intimately about my psychic experiences. At times all hell broke loose in my poor brain, and never, never had I thought that my turbulent psyche would want me to be exposed to the views of unknown people. I have lived a life hidden and unknown except to a few, a very few who often would soon forget the unorthodox part of my life; so that I would again appear as just another handsome gentleman and happy husband of distinguished background.

Now my Lord, my Self, you force me to bring to light my sojourn through this life, with the accidents and happenings of a soul most willing to hide what it knows. I fear that terribly. Why do you torture me out of my hiding, oh Lord? Why make me a spectacle to attract the present-day contempt of the so-called educated people? Why now the glare of daylight? Give me the darkness of the unknown, where I am safe and away from jealous dragons, hungry for the gold born of the pain of my tear-torn and trampled ego! Why can't I stay hidden so that I can soothe the last scars which hide the gashes? Why can't I wait until my skin safely covers my wounds? Power, power of the Unknown, why force me out into the open, away from the privacy of my own suffering, bearable only through the sweet love of my wife?

Oh, but I cry in vain, my voice is not heard, or it is heard and not heeded. Or is it heard, and smoothly and relentlessly put aside for a greater issue? Is the story again, as before, and now, and ever after, the sacrifice of the one for the many? Haven't I learned that lesson? Haven't I learned and listened to that ancient song of the human soul: one shall lead, and those who love will follow in his path? Is it my path to open the black wounds of darkness for the thousands of seekers? If so, where, oh Lord, is your ointment? Where is your healing salve? Will humanity suffer unto eternity? Is that why I now bring to the blinking eyes of the many my innermost secrets and happenings? This is a lament, not from the heart alone, not just from the head or feet. It is a lament from all of me, who in the outer world am Erlo van Waveren, born in Hillegom, Holland, son of the bulb merchant, Theodoor and his wife, Marie, from Amsterdam.

Tears, tears, but to no effect. Steadily, like a drum-beat slowly pulsating from distances far, far away in cosmic silence born comes the Word:

"Erlo, Erlo, bare yourself for your own protection. Help, help those who, like you, have suffered in darkness and do not know why. You have suffered the psychic pain of your eternal existence. You have been made aware of a consciousness in the Eternal Light. Darkness, with its deeper shadows, and its mystery and mysterious forebodings, has taught you a priceless lesson. Shine, shine, star of darkness and of light, unknown yet to those who go about groping, seeking, seeking everywhere for that which is *theirs* — their God, their Redeemer, their Self — sensed, surmised, but not as yet experienced.

"You know. You know for yourself concretely what has been the path of your experiences. They don't. They do not know. Their peculiar ways lead them astray in a world of rational miasma, and their souls go begging for an answer.

"Now start your record, as calmly and clearly as possible, about your dream life, and the life you have forced yourself to live as a well camouflaged seeker. A fool of God you are, but not of man. Write about your psychic life and the wonders it has brought you. From afar the drums and trumpets are sounding the hour of revelation of your myth, so that God and man may judge.

"Don't ever try to be understood. Don't ever try to achieve. Don't address any particular group of people. Tell your story, for if it is left untold, disaster will follow. This is not a threat, it is a truth. Tell your story to the tribe because the happenings of your life are too burdensome to be carried alone. Share it according to true American Indian tradition. Now go to bed, it is past midnight."

The next morning

THE SNOW has covered all the ugliness of our dirty town. The garden looks immaculately white and I am seated in the living-room overlooking the pretty picture of our small snowscape. What a relief it is not to work today! The chores have been done and I will now try to write as simply as possible.

Many strange bedfellows have come my way. They were attracted to me by a bond I wish I didn't have. In dreams, in dreamlike states, against my protests, they came out of darkness, revealing themselves in order to make me aware of a psychic state that was apparently waiting for clarification. It seems as if in my psyche nothing can come to rest until consciousness is capable of experiencing it with feeling and emotion. Painfully, these ancestors of my soul worked themselves into my fantasy world to take on different aspects of their characters, returning to life in this book to become reborn and integrated into this new age of Aquarius. Never, never had they thought to come back and live unlived, unresolved regions of their psyche. But Aquarius came and Gabriel sounded his trumpet and loudly announced the coming of the New Age, even unto the Netherworlds.

Paul, in his first epistle to the Corinthians, is just as profound and true now as two thousand years ago when he prophesied to his far-away flock: "Behold, I show you a mystery; We shall not all sleep, but we shall be changed, in a moment, in the twinkling of an eye, at the last trumpet: for the trumpet shall sound and the dead shall be raised incorruptible and we shall be changed."

Now the trumpets are being raised and their call heard by the living and the dead. And so my psychic ancestors came to me. It is as Paul wrote to his Corinthians: "For this corruptible must put on incorruption and this mortal must put on immortality."

In curious formation they came, like diamonds in a row. I saw them, involved in the resurrection of Jerusalem, no richer or truer city ever existed. To Jerusalem, the City of God, the seat of our eternal being, they went to undergo the revivification of their spirit. Through much travail they came. First through my psyche, then through the tale they spun with their magic lives, they brought to light the new spirit of Aquarius in me.

Aroused by the mana of the times, Wilfrid, the saint of York, the archbishop of the seventh century, came out of his grave. He had to become aware of what he had destroyed in primitive man of those ancient days in his beloved England by establishing Roman rule and ritual at the council of Whitby in 664. At that time, the beauty of England's pre-Christian spirit was violated and its wild naturalness was thrown into the pit of Hell under the altar of his Church. The civilized ritual of greater sophistication, based on the marvelous Gregorian spirit of Italy, was superimposed on those pagan children, to the greater glory of God and to the delight of Hell. For centuries to come, this darkening of pagan lights, this "cover-up" of Nature's magic, would create fierce battles in the Christian psyche which now have to be released, depotentiated and reinstalled as a vital, positive life-force. So Aquarius awakened Saint Wilfrid in the North Riding of York to make his pilgrimage into consciousness.

For the same reasons, and according to the laws of the Eternal Return, my spiritual ancestors reappeared to seek clarification of that which could not be lived or understood before by the limitations of their times and their incarnations. Thus appeared the powerful Walter de Gray, Archbishop of York from 1216 to 1255; the sophisticated François de Fénelon, Archbishop of Cambrai from 1695 to 1715; the undaunted Saint Asterius, Archbishop of Amasia, who lived the entire length of the fourth century, initiating the adoration of relics, and who wrote homilies that would again be much read five centuries later. My first Christian ancestor is Judas Barsabas, a prophet in his own right, and brother of the candidate for the place of Judas Iscariot. These men are my spiritual forefathers.

Then there is Kerl, an old Dutch word for the common man. I call him Kerel – the Lord Kyros. Kyros means Lord or master, so I take Kerel, Carl, Karel, Karoll, Charles as derivatives of the word Kyros, meaning, to me, the Lord Man. In my writing he represents all that man has ever lived through in our human experience. He is an aspect of the wise man, the one who knows all that has been lived. Kerel is the archetypal man in us all, that fount of information available to us when we are willing and able to listen.

The Hotel Schloss Ragaz
Bad Ragaz, Switzerland
July 27, 1966

THE EVENT of my birth is hidden from me in a twilight zone. It is not all darkness to me, not the black of the total unknown. It seems rather that I can recall faintly a terrific pull and attraction to Mother Earth, as if in the hidden crevices of tissues and sinews there would be for me a light of unknown beauty. My soul cried out in an agony of delight: "Make the plunge." This cry forced me to dive, and with a thundering crash of lightning I came through that mysterious wall which separates the worlds. I was born.

The experiences of the other side seemed removed. I was now enclosed in a box of feeling-flesh, sensitive to everything but aware of nothing except the moment of separation from all I knew, all I remembered of another universe of endless possibilities and bewildering vistas. I was caught by the Lord's call, which had catapulted me into this world with enormous power and will, and I was received by Earth with an equally powerful element of love. It seemed that the creative and the receptive, two all-important powers, had bound me to a giant shuttlecock, embedding me in the great design being woven in this cosmos.

At that moment of entrance, a terrible sense

of bewilderment overcame me, a chaotic moment in which all my values had to be realigned. My gravity became my body: my thoughts lost their power as if their wings had been clipped by a giant scissor. My mind twirled and twisted. It was as if my new body of flesh was now my only freedom. My spirit gave a desperate yell, which penetrated this new-found freedom as my very essence sensed the oncoming agony of being encased in a mortal body. The birth had succeeded.

Here I was on earth, catapulted, attracted, received, expected, in agony and bewildered, but seemingly full of purpose and obeying a thousand and one reactions and animal complexes, the greatest of which was love, good warm animal love of the mother body. Without that love the entire miracle of my coming would have ended in a dark hole of blackness, despair and death. The impact of birth, with its enormous archaic powers and rituals, its vast complicated laws, and deep, gripping emotions, was completely dependent on one factor. Could all this immensity be received and carried by the love of *my* mother? Not just the mother's love for the powers of life working through her, but love for *my* particular individual soul making its entrance into the world.

*Three days later
on July 30
in Bad Ragaz*

With my birth I had painfully broken the ties of love in a world of the beyond in order to establish my new being here on earth, to start a new cycle, a new beginning in the endless chain of Being. In one way, there would be no difference, for I live wherever I am. On the other hand, there was this immense new undertaking of returning. I was reborn in a new body, a new opportunity to mend the old ills and fears, and provide a new alive consciousness with which to continue the eternal round of living. After every dive into this earthly life, a new, more challenging beginning for the life hereafter is established. Then, as this new awareness on the other side becomes devitalized by its use, a return is made, a new descent into this world so that we may achieve the next goal in our eternal rounds. To experience, to fight, to become, to leave, and to return to this unique earth of ours is what the immense spirit of man needs and wants. For nothing is more vitalizing, nothing more rewarding to the soul than the apparent, but not actual, mire of our earthly experience. In this place of dense psyche, which is our earth, and with the *Prima Materia,* we live, we play, we manipulate, we experiment in order to find the light of consciousness. It is not to find out who we are, that matters, but *what* we are as human beings. Who we are is the mystery, perhaps gradually unveiled by what we are.

I feel that a myth is being evolved, as if the dreamer in me wanted to tell an ancient tale of the soul. I know from experience that the knowledge of the unconscious will voice truths which seem strange to the rational mind. However, if I refuse to accept these ideas, a part of my nature will be cut off. In any case, I have no choice; so I might as well stop fighting. Those ideas, those voices seek expression.

We are now in the Engadine Valley in Sils Maria, the place Nietzsche so loved It is August 5

A STRONG INNER voice speaks:

"The greatest difficulty, my dear Erlo, is your worldliness, a curious combination of several factors which was clearly shown to you in this morning's dream. It is absolutely necessary to give up the ego expression, and even the soul has to be pure of heart in order to receive the message of what Aquarius wants you to know. Your personal expression will come automatically because it is the only way you can receive the universal message which is now constantly beamed out and is responsible for your conflict. The old cannot comprehend the new. Now try to be that quality, that spirit you are, but without the peculiarities of the twentieth century. The material, rational world of today has to be thoroughly understood in order to be discarded. You are still trying to cut a figure in it as a psychologist or a writer with a masterwork to perform. However, let it be performed through you, whatever it is, and do not interfere with what *I* shall create. I am that

Mystery beyond Time, beyond human comprehension, not to be defined. Call me the Voice, the Self, the Void, Eros or Logos, or whatever you will — but do not ignore me. Give up the world and love me as the true source of that which is, was, and is to be. Now, write your farewell to the world, and try to do it tomorrow."

The next day
August 4
Sils Maria

ABOUT MY WRITING: Before any serious work is attempted, I must bid farewell to all that is in my world, even to my psychology of life. My twentieth century wall has to tumble. It is a death, a complete death which is involved. Can I ever do it? I will walk in the woods now, not alone, but with my darling wife, Ann.

On August 5
in Sils Maria
I wrote

THE GOODBYE

LORD, HELP ME! Once before, I said goodbye to my ego expression. It was perhaps the greatest agony I have ever experienced. I had worked hard and looked forward to a stage career, when my dreams indicated that I was a psychologist. The struggle to dare to be an actor had been so difficult after giving up the directorships of two old family concerns. Now, by writing this book, I know I must give up my own ideas regarding my contribution to psychology. I have been successful in it for so many years. People have trusted me, and I have been deeply devoted to helping those who came for advice. I had always hoped to do something in the world of my peers, to write a book, to teach or lecture; thus I would have given my contribution to the world of psychology and to the world of my friends. But now I say goodbye to this. That kind of ego satisfaction shall not be mine.

I also wanted acclaim from the world, and from the people who are making important contributions to this age. But goodbye to that as well. Goodbye to all my ego wishes for the admiration, affection and respect of my dear and beloved friends. All that is still animal vanity, like the pride of the wolf with a glossy coat. I go to a different land now, not by choice, but by life's will. Otherwise nothing can grow in me any more, even with the love and support of those nearest to me. I have to travel on, not further away, but deeper into a life I have not as yet experienced on earth.

For me, the difficulty of going on is the fact that I seem to leave behind a world in which I am not allowed to make my mark. I feel like a wayfarer who travels towards a goal but will always be a stranger to it. No one knows of me, and I have to leave my own circle before fulfillment. Nobody will know that I have lived, and no lasting product of my ego existence will be allowed.

But now my inner voice says: "It is not just a matter of giving up what you love. It is rather an uprooting of what you thought you could and really should accomplish. Even your psychic ancestors will never notice your worth until after the sacrifice of your ego. Before your expression is fulfilled, death comes."

Then where I will go is not important; it is beyond my comprehension. I fear to go into the oblivion, like Isaiah the Second. No one knows who he was; only what came through him. Through his sufferings, he extracted a universal truth to be used for ages to come. But can I stand such pain? Is my soul willing to go that road?

Where will I go and what will happen to me? I don't know, and it seems very unimportant. My death is all that matters, the death of my worldly knowledge as well as my spiritual knowledge. Ego and spirit are both at stake. The crucifixion must be complete — the death of any wish for expression, absolute. All this comes out of the deep conviction that nothing further can develop in me unless my ego — my brain, my mind, my ambition — all know and realize that Erlo as such is nonproductive and unimportant. Almost sixty-four years of effort, undone?

Now my inner being speaks: "Goodbye, my dear Erlo, goodbye. Oh, so many thanks for your efforts. I love your ambitions and all of your vanities. But please, please, oh please, do not come back! For if you return, all suffering is in vain. Your life, such as it was, would only turn into poisonous dust instead of the rock which it can become. This is true even if your life remains but a stepping stone for unknown feet, like the life of Isaiah the Second, the beautiful Egyptian known only to you and to me and remembered with the deepest love and affection." At this moment, I feel that I want a big, beautifully carved scarab over my heart and on my hand in remembrance of his life.

Now once again I have to disappear and enter into a development which entails my death.

"Die, Erlo! Go to your death with ~~my~~ YOUR tears as a blessing and my thanks. Go into oblivion, and leave all your desires and wishes. Drop them as a tree sheds its leaves so only that which is immortal remains. I know, you have but faint interest in immortality. That which is mortal tastes of this earth, which you did not know you loved so much. Have no desire left — be empty — be nothing — and see what happens. Walk in life as if you were an empty framework but pray to Heaven that the Devil does not enter; nor should there be any desires for the entrance of the Great."

With tears streaming down my face, and completely numbed by the total identification with my inner voice, I wrote the above.

Then the reaction came. The unknown will have to make a mighty proposition before I can continue on my task with any love or devotion. Life ahead is a vacuum, a Void, and that is needed, I suppose.

August 7
Sils Maria

You don't dare to give in to the greater idea, do you, Erlo? When you went to sleep, I told you, you are your own Redeemer. But, no, you knew better. You wake up and your heart is beating too fast. Still, you are the Redeemer. But, no, Erlo knows better. No one will descend for you. You are your own descent and ascent, your own Christ, your own Self. In you lies your own Redemption and Resurrection into self awareness and consciousness.

"The Redeemer is too great? Who or what else can there be but your own star, your own inner light. Is there a greater principle? Is there anyone else *now*, in the flesh, who could take on the role?

"Accept! Accept and find peace."

"Who cares who is the Redeemer? If I am, it will show. If I'm not, it will show. Foolishness of the unconscious. If my heart beats that much and is not at rest, tell me what it is I fight. . . .

"Well, then, I will not fight the idea of the Redeemer. Fine. That is it. I am. Then all anxiety can leave, for I have nothing to do any more; the Redeemer will have to live through me. . . .

"So I let go. Everything is fine. Erlo — *niente*. Redeemer is It. As you see, I am in different. But rest does not come to me. Perhaps in a while I will stop fighting the idea altogether. I will accept it from simple exhaustion, I suppose. . . .

"Is there still no relief? Well, then, I accept that I am, but what I am has to be proven. Perhaps this, perhaps that. I accept. But now, of course, you want me to accept the idea with love and warmth and human equilibrium."

"Erlo! Erlo! Erlo! You must realise that the spirit of the Redeeming Self is so great that it can write and speak the words of Christ and Buddha. These words brought light and comfort to the world. When the Redeemer is accepted and is alive in you, then the World Anima calls, and gods and ancestors claim their own."

"I realize that. But what within me fights it?"

"You'd never guess! Dress now, go out on the mountain; but walk slowly, and return to your room."

I did dress and walked through the beautiful larch woods of the Engadine, then came back to the hotel. And when I sat at my window, the following came.

"There is an entire Christian system of monks, priests, bishops and archbishops who are rebelling. They want to continue what was; they do not want to change. They were all so good, so hard-working, so insistent on Christian ways that you ought to talk to them, for they are all in an uproar. Their work is over and they hate it, but they have to be redeemed in order to be pillars of life's wisdom in the age to come. The pre-Christians within you don't bother you. The Christians do, and give you a terrible time, for they know that now they have to die and be reborn in you and they were so deliciously self-satisfied with their jobs."

August 8
Sils Maria

WELL, my dear old Christian ancestors, where are you? Fénelon, what is still on your mind, and my dear old scrappy Wilfrid, what is on yours? You two, and perhaps Judas Barsabas, are most perturbed. Asterius is happy because he can always participate in deep emotion, and Walter de Gray knows enough about the darkness of life not to be too delighted with Christianity. Asterius, will you come to my help? Wilfrid will be most upset because he loved and established the Roman Church in his England, and all his work has to be changed.

But now I hear Wilfrid's voice clearly, coming through all possible barriers. It is almost gruff and irritated.

"Arouse! Arouse! I hear it clearly. The trumpet sounds. I hear it, the trumpet, I hear it. Aroused I am, by your crude new spirit. Watch out! What harvest will that bring you: you disturb my beatitude, my soothing, healing influences, bringing peace and hope in a world of scandalous attitudes and vulgar behaviour. Why arouse me from the deep, benevolent sleep of my sainthood, from which I dispense my blessings to all who want to follow the spirit of the Lord Christ?"

I keep silent. I realize that the silence creates unrest in Wilfrid's aroused spirit. Then he continues:

"Is this the end of time for which I have waited so hopefully? I hear no peace in the trumpet. A shrill note and a syncopating rhythm forewarn me of a world I do not want to re-enter. And now, looking at you, awakener of the twentieth century, mouthpiece of the trumpet, I hesitate to open my lips again to start that fight which I won once, but which I cannot repeat, because my life does not flow that way anymore. I shudder and shake, seeing your bizarre clothing, your clown-like garb with long trousers and narrow fitting tunic. Who are you? Why confront me with your age of the future? I don't belong among your kind. I hear abominable noises of snorting and clanking metals around you. Leave — leave me, apparition, so that I can stay in my heavenly rest, in the realm of my peace-loving Christ where the birds mingled their voices with the angelic and the rustling feathers of divine wings beat the rhythmic drums of the Heavenly Choirs."

I answer: "Wilfrid, I hear your voice, and the agony in it which came with my presence. The echo of Gabriel's trumpet is with me, I know; that is my lot and my destiny. Forgive me if I disturb your heavenly rest, but I can be heard only by that part of your soul which lies listening, listening. Do you hear me? For centuries now, it has lain listening for the very sound you dislike, love, and long for. With me lies the redemption of all that could not be comprehended in your age, that looked-for, long-awaited power of the new enlightenment. Oh, I love you, Wilfrid, and all you did in your deeply moving life. In God's Hands rests the constantly rotating force of change, and with that the supreme opportunity for greater consciousness. All that could not be lived out, and was, and is still in your soul lies listening and does not come to rest until it has found its own world.

"You were never dead. You were slumbering and waiting for your Redeemer, and now you hear the trumpet of Gabriel the messenger. You hear him because your time of redemption is at hand. Not that you sinned so much, no indeed, but in living fully what you were meant to live, you have a spot of not-knowing, a dark field in the brilliance of your life achievement. All that we are, and all that we are not, both have a place. All achievement is limited by its very creation, and all creation of any kind has a shadow side. That shadow side that, not-knowing, is our teacher, and that teacher of the dark unknown is our Redeemer."

"Go away, you rascal! I know what I did better than you! I know the world well, and you can't tell me that the prisons and dungeons have disappeared. The greed, the narrowness, the jealousies of my century, I am sure, are flowering abundantly in your new age. Go away! And take that part which you say only slumbers. Go, I say!

"No, no, no, don't go! There is a pain in my heart, a spasm, a cramp which belies my peaceful state. This pain, just now, penetrates me. What is happening? A deep uneasiness, I sense. I thought I had put it to sleep at my death. The church choirs drowned my unresolved uneasiness, which I now feel again. Erlo, I must speak, listen! Now, after all these years, I sense a strange phenomenon, a new awareness. They said that I was awkward, that I was brusque and too forceful. Accused I am of not listening to my contemporaries and brusquely overriding them with my own and mostly better opinions. These primitive country bumpkins trying to deal with matters of the Church were often an abomination to me. But, curiously enough, I sense an uneasiness. Could it be that I was unwilling to understand such primitive mentality or ignorance? And haughtily went ahead?"

I answer: "What makes you say this now? Is that the story of your heart? Is that the sudden pain of a hidden truth which could not surface until now?"

"What do you want from me, Erlo? I don't like what you say. I feel pained. It is an uncomfortable awakening, another field, another world far from my blissful state of . . ."

"Ignoring a truth," I bluntly interrupt. Wilfrid looks at me with his grey-green eyes. His well shaped mouth and his long, inquisitive nose, in fact all his features, are now sharply brought out; not a part of him is left out of focus to my eyes. He stands proudly, defiantly, stamping his staff. My God, I think, what a dear child of God, what a spoiled youngster he is.

Wilfrid is furious. He raises his crosier, which turns suddenly into a huge, long trumpet. It emits a groan that intensifies into the clearest penetrating note, shattering forever Wilfrid's sleep of innocence and ignorance. Shuddering as if in a fever, he hands me the symbol of his shepherd's role which has become the awakener of his soul: "Take this from me, it has turned against me. I am no longer the one I was and made of myself.

Peace has fled from me and doubt is my companion."

His quick mind suddenly turns on me:

"Erlo, what made you come?"

"Aquarius, I suppose."

"Who is he?"

"The new shepherd who will unite the unknown with the known. From where that came out of me, I don't know, but nothing in me wants to change it."

"Where does he come from?"

"Out of me, and the pain of your heart, Wilfrid."

Wilfrid listens intently, then asks: "Is he — is he — a man of sorrow?"

"That is how he announced himself to you, and that is how he entered your consciousness."

"Pain, pain, oh God, deliver me from more pain." He puts his left hand on his heart and it slowly travels down his spleen to his hips where it rests. "Pain, pain, I must be back on earth again, pulled into another focus, another awareness of my heart. Oh, sweet Jesus, have mercy, have mercy, for in this land of the earth in which we are all sinners, I don't want to live any more. In the name of the Trinity and all that is Holy, don't let me return to earth without a greater Light, a greater help! Neither do I want to live a repeat, another fight for the glory of God, another campaign against the slothful man, the sluts, the slander, the pathetic ignorance of jealousy, the intolerance — none of that.

I refuse, I rebel, I won't, I can't! Back to my haven, back to my rest, back to oblivion if need be, but not any more what was. Oh God, no more of what was!"

I listen to the desperate saint of the past, and not a word of comfort escapes my lips. Nothing comes to my help. The despair is too complete, too overwhelming. I must respect this deep suffering. Curiously enough, it seems to ennoble my heart. What a dichotomy! Such stark suffering should not be made cheap by my comfort. It is so true that it will find its own way in God's spirit, and thus it will create its own answer.

Wilfrid turns away and thinks of all his travail. A powerful wave of memory engulfs him. He looks at the roots of his personality with the questioning mind of an Aquarian.

"Was my work for nothing? Did I start all these monasteries out of vanity? Was I so wrong in doing away with the Pagan mysteries?"

"No, no," I answer, "it all had to be done then, but this is another time."

"My congregation, my flock, they still pray for me," says Wilfrid, "I hear them. I can even hear the bells in the church towers. They still call the people to prayer and they still implore me to be the bridge to Christ. And I still answer their calls. Am I to shut them out and ignore them?"

"No, Wilfrid, answer their calls, but don't continue to hold humanity to the orthodox forms any longer. Support their real needs, but don't restrict your followers to the old rules. The New Ways have more freedom and include the Dark as well as the Light. Evil is not to be despised, but suffered and understood.

"Oh, dear Wilfrid, thank you. Thank you for all

the good works you have done and for the things done in your name. Visit the churches and tell them about the new tidings of tolerance. Tell them that Christ has His shadow, or Dark Brother, and that the Dark Brother, Judas Iscariot, is God's being also. The new consciousness can come only through that recognition."

Wilfrid does not want to hear this.

"Will they stop praying for me?"

"Do you mean praying for you or to you?"

"As they prayed, I was so proud and felt holy."

"Wilfrid, you rascal, there lies your vanity. The aeon is over. Your holiness must come to its end, as you ended the life of the pagan Gods. But, like them, you can live in golden memory if you accept the Shadow of God, of Christ, of Jesus, and so allow the new to enter as you did before."

"I know," Wilfrid answers, "I know. The Shadow of Christ is very hard for me to accept. I have helped to fight it for so long. I know I am fighting the acceptance of all the shadow part of life. But do I have to say goodbye to "my Christ," to that world of infinite beauty and spirituality? It is as if I see nothing but blackness ahead of me, but I know I can face it when I stay connected with the Light of Christ. And the Mass — it was so beautiful. I did all I could to enlarge it and glorify it. Do I say goodbye to that too?"

"Yes, to its form, but not to its magic, nor to Christ, for that great spirit should never be denied. Be all-inclusive and welcome Light and Darkness, each in turn as they come. But judge both! In that lies your power now, and your gift to God."

"I will try, but centuries of custom are not easily set aside."

"If you don't follow the New, dear Wilfrid, there is an inevitable curse on you for preventing the living spirit of Aquarius from coming through. Now let us pray and meditate and say farewell to your beloved churches as you remember them. But please, oh please, relinquish your vanities, your personal longings, and all that stands between you and the spirit of Christ with his Dark Brother."

While praying, we are transported imperceptibly to Ripon, Wilfrid's favorite church in Yorkshire. On the altar, I plant a wooden black cross, upside down, next to the cross already there. Wilfrid, remembering his great fights for the rights of Rome, at first feels devastated that he has to listen to another authority, which is not from the Pope or the Church, but from a human being. He looks at me and, while our eyes meet, his heart starts to beat wildly, because, deep in his bowels, it rumbles. "The authority lies within you and not outside in a church. Stay true to your nature, kiss the altar, say goodbye and be a trailblazer. You are and were born that way."

Slowly, Wilfrid accepts the inevitable. He knows his inner voices. He turns around and embraces the columns of his church. It is as if, with his newly acquired wisdom, he were pulling down its ancient structure. Then, with a shudder, he seems to shake off the past. I quickly take Wilfrid by the arm and talk animatedly about the changes of the time, for, suddenly, I cannot bear the idea of that ancient holy place being undone by our modern thoughts. I do not know who is more afraid. Wilfrid seems less disturbed than I. His trail-blazing spirit is still with him, apparently, and at this moment I am more fearful than he is about the undoing of the past.

My incessant, almost forced conversation keeps Wilfrid occupied on our way to Harrowgate, where we enter the modern church built in his honor and say our prayers at its altar. Here Wilfrid is deeply moved. He gropes for his new roots and asks for the acceptance of Christ and His Shadow and the recognition of the new Light. Listening in bewilderment are the spirits of the past and present. Is this their Saint Wilfrid, they wonder? He begs his spirit congregation to help him and thus themselves. Moving slowly through the multitude which is gathering around him, he murmurs: "Pray for your soul, pray for your soul and remember the dark night which brought redemption. Remember the crucifixion with its glorious resurrection. Don't deny the darkness its power which the Christ turned into God's light." Thus, speaking as if in a trance, he leaves the church.

At the side portal, he looks back and makes the sign of the cross over his congregation. As always, Wilfrid is looking for solutions in the very center of authority. He grasps the fact that it is now not Rome but the city of God which must provide. So he addresses his followers.

"I am on my way, on my pilgrimage to the seat of my own soul, Jerusalem, the City of God, and advise you, my beloved congregation, to do the same." At that very moment, a Light emerges in the church and lights up the spirit of all those around. As each takes a part of that Light for guidance in search of his own soul, they file out in deepest silence. The church becomes an empty shell.

SADLY WE LEAVE them to continue our journey to the mighty Minster of York, the seat of Wilfrid's archbishopric. As Primate of England, he is made welcome by one of his successors, the powerful Walter de Gray, thrice Regent of England. The tall, majestic archbishop rises out of his sleep wearing the splendorous robes in which he was laid to rest. On his hand glitters the enormous ring with emeralds clutching an opal. The golden lions on his silk bandolier show clearly as he opens his arms wide to embrace his ancestor. As he does so, he awakens from his trance-like state and becomes aware simultaneously of Wilfrid's bewildering journey from Ripon. At the same time, the plan for the pilgrimage to Jerusalem is revealed to him.

The proud bishop senses a new wavelength. Oh, how he hates unknown forces. They can only be wicked and his own blackness, so well concealed during his lifetime, jumps to the fore.

"Out!," he roars at me, imperiously pointing to the doors. "Out, you blasphemer, undoer of Christ's will!"

A peal of laughter escapes my throat. I also roar, but with laughter. Wilfrid is baffled at how I handle this hostility.

"Out!", shouts Walter again, less loud and imperiously. But nothing in me moves.

"Walter," I say, "calm down. Come down from your throne and remember the times when your ill-placed authority didn't call on Christ's will. Follow Wilfrid's example and listen to *your* inner authority. Give up your fears and stay with your deathbed resolutions. You asked for understanding and compassion. Try to be as humble as you were then. Don't let your fear of my new authority bring you back to your weakness."

Walter looks at me with incredulity. He is so taken aback that he does not realise that, during our spat, a chain has mysteriously appeared, linking the wrists of Walter and Wilfrid. It is a light chain made of wrought iron, and I am subsequently joined in the same way to them. Like three holy pilgrims of unavoidable doom, we move now toward the main altar, to pray, to say good-bye.

I feel Walter pulling at his chain so hard that it hurts my wrist. Suddenly, he yanks sharply and stands still. "Not so fast, stranger," he says to me. "I will not undo so soon what I built up. Little do you know how hard I fought to achieve my worldly wealth. I enriched this church with priceless treasures. I built the church of Ripon almost anew. Thrice I ruled the land for the King. It took all my cunning and strength to establish my bishopric on a permanent basis so that no King with greedy hands could interfere in our church properties. No tampering now with my church. No debacles, no doom. The old spirit suffices for me."

There he stands, champing at the bit, that extremely tall man, almost six feet four, a magnetic personality, with unusual brown eyes and flaring nostrils. What a figure! This time, I don't laugh, fully realising the shock of the awakening and the seriousness of my visit with its devastating powers.

"Come along, Walter, you and I as well as Wilfrid are in the grip of the unalterable spirit of the New Times." I feel for him and it is in my voice. Slowly, I start to walk again. "What awoke you, Walter?," I ask.

"Don't ask, don't ask, I don't want to recall my waking dream. It was frightening, and those trumpets, those trumpets!"

Now there is silence; only our shuffling feet are heard on the stones of the vast edifice. But Walter has to speak, he has to share with us; it is too much for him to carry the awakening by himself.

Agitatedly, he begins again: "That haunted dream vision! While still half asleep, I saw wildly galloping horses coming across the green hills, men and women mounted, some blind, some naked, fiercely swinging their arms. Hair flying, like furies they came. Then they suddenly halted in front of a crucifix beside a narrow path, overshadowed by an ancient tree — oh, no, don't," Walter moans, tears rolling down his cheeks. But he has to continue: "They tore ... they tore the Christ from the cross. Their hands were bleeding. It was as if each were wearing His thorny crown, and blood streamed down their faces. Oh, God! They prayed and shouted: "Lord, descend into us. The earth is parched, only our feet can make the soil fertile again, when we are imbued by you." At that, the earth flamed up as if the spirits of the underworld had risen. And there was a union of man, spirit and earth and my bowels groaned.

"Oh God, have mercy, oh Lord, have mercy. Mary, Mary, Mother of Christ, bestow your wonders on my being."

Walter leans against a pew. His hand moves across the wooden curves as though he could wring help out of that wood.

Wilfrid and I look at each other, perplexed and moved, for here is another story of the coming of the New Age, with all its wild untamed forces, a cry from the hidden soul, coming over the horizon like a sun throwing its first light in search of salvation.

I don't talk; I sigh and my eyes brim over. Wilfrid heaves a sob and says: "Come on, Walter, you have told us the way. The flame of earth has to meet the Christ, and the bloodbath is as unavoidable as the pilgrimage to our salvation." Walter looks at us. He cannot yet comprehend all, but, relieved by his communing, he follows, disarmed. No fight is left in him. Slowly, we proceed, laden with the bitter reality of the awakening dream-vision.

The stones again echoing our steps, Walter, touching each pew as we proceed, begins anew: "Wilfrid," he says, "I want to talk with you. I feel, when I speak to you, that I am speaking to a father, perhaps to the great ancestor." He smiles. "I am not sure I know Him, but He must be in my blood and I feel I can touch him if I tell you about my life. Perhaps then I will know more about the purpose of my travail."

We stand now in front of the altar steps, and it

comes to me that the thirteenth century did not speak much, if at all, about the Ancestor. I can't help smiling as it becomes obvious that another spirit is already entering into Walter.

While observing this, we mount the steps. Three chairs miraculously appear and we seat ourselves in them. I look at the altar and notice that a shadowy outline of a figure is leaning against the ancient sacrificial stone, partly hiding the cross from me. Then I hear Walter's voice again: "Wilfrid, you must know that I built a shrine for you. I remember so well holding your skull in my hands, thinking of you, and feeling you even in my bones. When I put it to rest, it made me think of an apple fallen from a tree. I admired your life and its tenacity. I prayed to you, for you — not knowing you are part of me. That knowledge rises up now, as if it were an old truth, and it gives me an inner peace."

He pauses a while, cherishing that new, wonderful truth. Smilingly, he continues: "I worked well and I lived well. I enriched my family and my church, and I was the Church. Many times did I travel as ambassador for good King John." The "good" surprises him and makes him smile. "I was three times Regent of England for his son, King Henry, who knew I was a good organizer and could squeeze out provisions for his army in France. I loved the boy, but did not like him, always.

"Born ambitious, the hard blows of life made me cunning. I have been called avaricious; perhaps it is true but I don't feel it that way. I can be tough, but, now, telling this, I realize that I had to learn to wield power, to taste it, to become aware of what that power does to others and, above all, what that power does or did to me. Frankly, you can never become detached from this world or evaluate it properly until you have experienced its riches. That haughty, priestly attitude of phony simplicity has no value when it is just withdrawal from life. I can't see the magic in that. I lived richly and loved it. Not until I was older did I comprehend the meaning of simplicity; only then could my ambitious side taste other realities. My true spirit entered on my death; it was pure joy and put the struggles of my earth life in perspective. In the annals, they say that, at the end, I was weak in my brains. I was not; never was I clearer. First I suffered deeply, agonizingly, as I spoke to my soul. The earth had taken my spirit, and then given it back. I became free and my spirit soared. I died happily and peacefully. You have no idea of the relief, the immense relief. My task was done.

"Your life, your times were so different, Wilfrid. I am a child of the Magna Carta. When I rode out with King John from Windsor, little did I suspect that I would spend the last days of my life in parliament trying to teach the nobles the rules of that game. There was no more cunning or greed left in me. Service became natural, but what a long road I had had to travel! In my soul, Wilfrid, there must have been a memory of your troubles with rough kings. John most unroyally sold my estates while I was his ambassador to France. He needed the money to pay the Pope for my bishop's seat in York. When I came back, I was York, surrounded by much glory and pomp; the King had more power in the church and I was as poor as Job." Walter smiles almost maliciously. "But not for long. Whatever they say about me, I did not impoverish my flock, the estates were well taken care of. Of course, my family got richer, but those were hard times.

"When John died, Henry was crowned and I anointed him, well do I remember. My privileged position to the crown tipped the scales. Greed and power took control. I trusted neither man nor beast. It was as if I had taken root in the cunning of the times. I loathed the regents of Henry III. I wanted to outsmart them, but in my way. The occult always had great interest for me, and so I decided . . ."

But Walter could not continue. Then, after a while, he spoke again. "I was, I am an archbishop. That means the apostolic blessing is carried by me. It is the greatest treasure given to me, perhaps the only true jewel there is, and now . . . Oh, my God, I feel low, very low." He slumps in his chair, his knees seek the ground and he drops to the altar floor, a crumpled figure. After a while, he calmly and almost majestically gets up. Standing straight, he speaks without a trace of pity for himself. "You know, Wilfrid, I confessed this once; but now you are here and, on my right, this new version of our spirit with his trumpeteer, and so I have to repeat my confession to the past and the future.

"My very darkest nature forced me even to say the black mass in order to get power over the young King. Thank God, I failed. I suppose that the blessings of Him whom I carry counteracted my poisonous self. Thrice did I say that mass; it haunted me and, in the end, purified my existence. I have lived it out painfully. But my inner being suffers it still.

"Telling this makes me understand more about my vision of this morning: the incoherent darkness of the soul has to be redeemed. The time has come for another Darkness, but black it is. The ignorance of evil is still its tool. I know that power in me and I accept it. God grant me strength to suffer it into awareness, wherever I am." At that, two large tears of blood drop on the altar.

Walter sees them. He turns towards me: "Let us proceed, Erlo. I knew your name but could not bear pronouncing it before. Let us proceed and accept the times which have awakened me. My incomplete self, my questing soul I will follow throughout the ages. I know about my immortality and I never lived it. Now I do."

We proceed to the altar and kneel in prayer. Next to the golden cross standing in the middle, I install a second one of black corroded silver. It makes Walter shiver. He holds on to Wilfrid, and the three of us start on our way to the south transept, where we entered. It is as if I have to pull those two powerful bishops along.

Suddenly, a clatter. The chains are broken. I turn around and see Walter and Wilfrid disappear into one of the enormous columns. I stand unshackled and alone in the huge cathedral. The Stones of the column then speak with their voices. First a whisper, then a thundering voice declares: "We are the Church; we stay here. We are the

Light; we shun the Shadow."

A black-winged thought of the Preserver, that powerful Lord of cosmic order, has gripped the soul of my companions. That unyielding aspect of God has taken hold of my friends. In that stifling moment, creation or destruction come to naught. All is as ever and forever. It is a truly holy attempt to preserve what is, a counteraction to all the shocking events — a self-preservation which will not work, though we try and have a powerful ally. But we cannot change the moment or stop the natural flow of the new breath of life.

But I too am stifled. I try to remain with the known: this also is instinctive. The fear of the unknown in me is so great, I know it so well. I pray to the Lord Preserver to bestow on us the memories of the past in an indelible way so that nothing be lost of our journeys on earth or even in heaven. I pay my tribute to that benign power which also gives us the mercy of rest so that we may continue. I reach out to the stones in the column. I stroke them and feel with my ancient friends the shock we have had. First, I think there is nothing for me to do but go my way. But how can I, without them?

As I stand irresolute, I see that, slowly, the stones take on form again. The two men stand before me. Reluctantly, they emerge from the column, kneel before me and say: "We want to stay." They are like two youths, contrite and unwilling to mature. I want both of them with me and I cannot leave them behind. They embrace each other and, once again, disappear into the stones, but this time through the floor. Then they arise in back of me, tears streaming down their cheeks. I feel as if they are now in my aura, like a psychic backbone. Together, we ceremoniously kiss the floor the walls and wave to the altar.

Slowly leaving the cathedral, we are accompanied by a host of angels and the sound of great music from the organ and chorus singing a last Te Deum. Then, as Walter and Wilfrid precede me, the spirits of the past and present gather about us, bow, kneel and wave tearful goodbyes. Their tears are for the departing saints and leaders of their church. Now they stand painfully on their own. I feel that they, too, will go on their lone pilgrimage. In the large doorway of the transept Walter had built, we turn around and, with both doors open wide, we kneel to pray for the future of the Church — if there is to be such a thing. Suddenly two — no, one little devil appears out of the ground, a remnant spirit from the crypt. He kisses Walter and embraces Wilfrid. He is to stay behind.

But now, from nowhere, Kerel appears, the mighty Kyros, personification of all that man has experienced since time immemorial. He is truly a breath-taking figure — fully six feet tall, with a lionesque head, a wide forehead, piercing eyes which cannot hide the suffering of mankind, and a generous mouth. He stands in utter self-composure. Pointing at the little devil, he says: "Take that little fellow with you. The break has to be complete and forever." At that fierce command, the huge cathedral cracks and crumbles. The thunderous rumble is bone-chilling. It is the end. It is God's command, the spirit of the times functioning through the presence of those who are called upon.

I sway from the impact of this debacle; still, I feel slightly comforted by the nearness of Kerel. The great bishops, however, move away in utter horror. I look back sadly on the column of dust which rises slowly heavenward from the rubble. Wilfrid and Walter cannot. They stare ahead, hopelessly shaken by what has happened. I see Kerel entering the chaos of stone pillars, broken walls and windows. Then, in the middle of that havoc, he stretches his arms heavenward in supplication. I hear him ask: "Lord, will there be an answer to this?"

Our pilgrim's path now leads toward that difficult stumbling block of their ambitions, Canterbury, the mighty fortress of English spirituality. Wilfrid does not even like the mention of that name because it brings back so many controversies, so much unhappiness. Thank God there was a Rome to rule over it, he thinks.

Walter smiles grimly. Canterbury never allowed him to annex Scotland. He would have loved the title of Primate of England and Scotland, almost more imposing than Canterbury's title of Primate of all England. His eyebrows rise for a moment at the thought of all that vanity. "Who knows, it is still in me," he sighs. I look contentedly at my companions. We are now on horseback, the ancient knightly way of traveling.

The town of York disappears behind the horizon. We go farther and farther through the medieval woods and green pastures of this emerald island. Something makes me look back. The column of smoke of York's cathedral is now a dark cloud traveling with us like a shadow companion.

We have been a long time in the saddle. Apparently, our psyches are not so very anxious to proceed. I notice that our horses are trotting slowly. Then they start to walk almost lazily. We make no attempt to hurry them on. Now we go through a meadow path, over the hill, and there it lies, Canterbury with its magnificent towers and spires. I take a deep breath of the clear air and sigh. The horses sense our uneasiness and apprehension, and seem reluctant to carry us any farther. We dismount on a grassy slope outside the town as if, in that way, we could protect God's house of stone from any debacle.

There is no chapel or wayside station so we kneel on the grass. God's creation is our church. The heaven above is spotlessly blue and the earth's incense is the fragrance of the wild flowers. It is the Creator's earth and heaven, and ours. We pray for the union of earth and heaven so that a marriage may take place in our souls that will unite the Darkness of the earth with the Heavenly Light. We pray for another marriage of Adam and Eve, but, this time, with the blessing of the Creator. Deeper we go into prayer. I sense the stillness of soul in my two bishop brothers; it penetrates my heart and puts it in a deep rest. I sigh and sigh again as peace descends into my being. At that moment, we hear a fearful rumbling in the earth as it heaves with a terrifying sigh, like a panting breast. The heart of God seems to beat faster inside his immense earth body. Cracks appear in the land and thunder is heard. A faint smell starts to emanate from beneath us and, as we continue to pray in deepest fear of the Lord, we see from afar the toppling walls of mighty Canterbury. The roof falls, towers sway, windows break and a huge rocket of fire rises heavenward, bursts, and disperses itself in a sickening stench. The cathedral crumbles; tiny pieces of black grit fall at our feet — souvenirs for the pilgrims of the future.

Stunned by the devastation and awed by the might of the new powers around us, Walter, Wilfrid, and I leave and travel on to the Channel. They both know that, when they make the crossing, there will be no return to their England. Both of these men have ruled the land as kingly priests; they look back to say farewell to their former domains, but even more to say farewell to their deeply loved country, to which they have given their lives. They are true patriots with profound compassion for their homeland.

AROUSED FROM HIS SLEEP, François de Salignac de la Mothe-Fénelon, Archbishop of Cambrai, tutor to the Duke of Bourgogne, author, philosopher, educator, religious advisor to the court of Louis XIV — and an exile in Cambrai — is awaiting the wayfaring bishops, his English ancestors. His noble French seventeenth century mind is wondering what will happen.

All his full and distinguished life, he carried the sweet, gentle beauty of the Dordogne in his heart. That gentleness is of his essence and is his strength; with that, he faced his exile and the rebukes of his enemies. And with the same fortitude and sweetness of soul, he now awaits the arrival of Wilfrid and Walter. The spirit of the times has made him aware, by its unseen power, that his existence is not yet over. Something unfulfilled needs completion. The dawning consciousness of the age of enlightenment, of which he is so proud, is not enough for the time at hand.

Rubbing his eyes and shaking his head, he tries to understand the message but feels only apprehension and bewilderment as he hears and even vaguely sees — like a moving panorama — the events which happened to his brethren. He sees the upside-down cross and the black one. Like a flash, it occurs to him that Peter was crucified that way; well might that ancient, strange symbol be emphasized. But, as usual, he tries to reason and understand with only that part of his heart which readily accepts all gentlemanly understanding and abhors and shuts out all vulgarity of spirit. The dignity of the Catholic church is the measure of his heart.

As he moves to the south portal of his cathedral to welcome his visitors, he experiences a vision of Wilfrid and Walter — just their four eyes, with four or five tears of blood. They seem to express a depth of suffering he has never experienced himself. He quickly returns to his sanctuary, aware that this vision is not just a fantasy, but a deadly truth which is about to hit him. Neither the cultured façade of his seventeenth century nor his rigorous obedience to Rome's rule, which had so penetrated his being, would suffice to meet the power about to confront him. These attitudes of the past would act as poison to the unity of Light and Shadow.

Fénelon rushes to his bishop's throne and seats himself. Dressed in simple priestly robes, he anxiously awaits Walter and Wilfrid's arrival. The moment of revelation is upon him. The end of his world is near, a world which is more complicated and rational, less primitive than theirs. But François possesses the capacity for true suffering which has always enhanced his world with a beauty and sensitivity rare for a man of such culture and elegance. He deals with life in utter spiritual refinement. But these orientations alone are not enough to support life as it is lived now. His bulwark is the love of his people: "Mais le peuple m'adore," he thinks. Somewhere he is still vain, and he knows it.

Somehow, I cannot talk with François. He is so close to me that a dialogue cannot take place. My vision, my fantasy are his. We are like one and I am sucked into an area of my psyche where I am powerless. I must identify with this bishop of the early eighteenth century. I suffer with him; my duality of consciousness has ceased to be. I am like Fénelon. I AM – oh my God – Fénelon. There is no separation. I was he and I am he. He is alive in me – what a thing to accept. I might as well write "I" instead of François. Still, I am Erlo – and also François.

François turns his head towards the altar so that he will avoid witnessing the magical entrance of his ancestors, powerful men in the affairs of Church and state. They have gone through the whole debacle of their churches, and now his turn has come. Not only does he sense it, he knows it. He does not dare to turn around, but he realises that the doors of the cathedral are open. He stands up and goes to the altar in order to keep his back toward the pilgrims, and to pray for the last time to the single Christ, His Glory, His Light. There is no Shadow, only Light, His Light.

Now, in his most beautiful robes, but with the heart of a simple priest, Fénelon prays, hoping perhaps to forestall his fate. "Goodbye, Lord Christ, Glory of Light, only begotten Son of the Most High!" There is no music. The organ is silent, no cry is heard except that of the lost priest. It is his last devout, truly holy attempt to call on God's son Jesus: "Have mercy, oh Lord, pity my heart, where Jesus Christ founded my home. Do not destroy my Light, which gave me the strength to carry my life with fortitude. Spare my cathedral — my church, the mother of my congregation, and don't, I pray, disrobe my soul of its garment. What else can protect me from the rigors of life? In my weakness, I need your help for survival. Only begotten one of the Most High, I beg you, listen to this supplicant. Don't leave me, oh Lord Jesus, have mercy, Lord have mercy!"

François resembles a man taken from the cross with bleeding wounds and a lost soul. Then a vision comes to life, he sees his Christ dethroned, an emptied cross, — no cross. And then, oh God, it happens. The altar bursts open. From it a black cloud rises, and out of stark darkness two men emerge — one all Light and one all Dark. They embrace, entwine and clasp hands to signify the new powers rising out of the ancient altar. Now Darkness and Light are one and indivisible. The New Age is here. Christianity is dead.

I BURST INTO TEARS, can't write a word. This death is too much to take. What will happen? Centuries of unsolved life are upon me. My support is gone; I stand alone. Now I look at François in a different way. I see him devastated but within me.

There is, however, in me a core, educated differently, already immersed in another spirit so I am set free from my beloved Fénelon. My tears dissolve the total identification and, gradually, I come to the place where I can write again. Now the scene in the church opens up clearly before my mind's eye.

Wilfrid and Walter, who have traversed the long apse of the church while François was praying, put their arms around his waist. There they stand, taking in the awesome apparition, Walter on the left, François in the middle and Wilfrid, shadowy from agony and fear, on his right. They kneel with bowed heads knowing this is the revelation they seek; this is the New Moment, the life to come. No music. No organ. Only the dead silence of the awful birth. Then a howling note of cosmic agony booms through the church. All becomes more vibrant.

François shudders; he can't bear the sight of

this new image of God. He turns around and so witnesses his debacle. The church walls dissolve into a column of dust. The cathedral is dust. Wilfrid and Walter see only the apparition, the entwined brothers of Darkness and Light, the new symbol of power and wholeness. François slowly turns again, trying to accept the new Light, this altar-born vision of what-is-and-always-was, even before Christ. Gradually the connection with his rational mind is coming back. It occurs to him that the idea of the vision, while shocking and disturbing, is otherwise quite logical and clear.

At that moment, Kerel appears again, because François attempts to intellectualize the true meaning of the vision instead of emotionally reacting to its power. This rationalist attitude would dry up the forces of the living spirit. "To hell with your spirit-killing intellect!", Kerel shouts, and with a powerful sweep of his arm, the last root of François' rational attitude is pulled out and laid to dry on the debris of the church floor.

François shivers as if a wind were blowing through him and stripping him of his clothing. Sobbing, he falls to the floor as the new spirit of the vision enters him. Wilfrid and Walter come to his help and, as they lift him to his feet, the three experience a quickening and deepening of the understanding and powers of the mighty new Holy Ghost.

In a flash of recognition, François becomes aware of a new disposition, another attitude towards life. His long career of educating the royal princes, the noble ladies — the sophisticated snobs of the intelligentsia — passes through his head. He becomes painfully conscious of the one-sidedness of his beloved Church. He recalls his sermons and his letters, always emphasizing nobleness of thought and action while turning a half-deaf ear and a blind stare to the importance of all that and those lost in the darkness of the devil's grip. "Oh God, will I ever embrace that darkness with enough love and compassion for its redemption? How much I have to learn and understand!" He crosses himself in the name of the Father and the Son and the Holy Ghost, and adds slowly "and the Holy Mother." No more Trinity alone; the power of the earth has to be included.

Kerel, deeply satisfied with this change, stands in the midst of the crumbled church surrounded by rubble and dust. He is the pillar of the past, and the clearing house of life and death for the development of the Self. There is no music and he can almost hear the silent passing of time. All that is orthodox in the archbishops, all the inevitable limitations of their times are vanishing. The three, in total exhaustion, accept their fate and, in so doing, unite in consciousness with Kerel. Through this union, the greater clarity of Kerel becomes part of them. His wisdom will now be available to their soul.

The Man of Light and the Man of Darkness, still clasping hands, turn toward Kerel as they descend from the altar, thus setting foot on earth for the first time. What they touch is the dust, the *prima materia* out of which their future church will have to be built.

Kerel genuflexes reverently to the newborn

spirit, turns, and looks at the holocaust. Intensely moved, he picks his way through the aperture where once the great doors gave entrance to the church. The wide open landscape in front of him, the flatlands of Northern France, shows nothing but endless bleakness. Far in the distance is their next beacon on this devastating but holy pilgrimage, Rome. Kerel leads the way, followed by François, Walter, Wilfrid, then me, and, behind us, the two Sons of God, the two Christs next to each other, clasping hands.

It is a great moment in time. What will happen to Rome, the seat of supreme authority, where the throne of Saint Peter has been occupied for centuries by his successors? What will our presence do to that glorious city?

August 9
Sils Maria

A<small>ND</small> so I watch with my inner eye. There they go, first Kerel, then François and Walter next to each other and, falling behind, Wilfrid, the least willing and the most sad. He almost disappears in a mist, but he has to go along. He experienced the Christ in the first millenium and overcame evil so many times in his life that to accept the Dark Son of God still seems sheer folly to him. "Oh God," Wilfrid sighs, "couldn't I have stayed asleep, untouched by time? Your power, Your kingdom, oh Lord, is more than weird. Now to know that Darkness and Light are expressions of one nature is too overwhelming. Both Your Will and Glory make me fear You all the more."

Wilfrid looks back and sees again the dual figures of the two Sons of God — only now they are surrounded by a glow of soft light. This image is to follow and become part of them, as inseparable as a cloud is to rain. In this manner, they travel on.

I see them now, crossing the land of François, beautiful France. It is his country. So many of his ancestral family fought here, and had their glories, defeats and capers. François is France, as Wilfrid and Walter are England. François is well aware of the many, many connections which bind him to this country. The Gramont, the Montmorency, the Salignac, the de la Motte-Houdancourt, the Bourbon, and many more soul connections slumber in his heart. During this pilgrimage, he integrates the mana of these many lives lived with such intensity. All this rises up in François' mind and strengthens his backbone. Then another powerful wave of memories comes over him. He recalls the papal authority; he thinks of his defeat in Rome and the Pope's fear of Louis XIV. He remembers that, in a way, he wanted to be a cardinal; he knows he deserved the honor. He does not condemn the Pope, but feels a great sadness about the whole miserable Bossuet affair, his defeat by that powerful Bishop of Meaux. He is almost morose for a moment as he recalls that the powers of the spirit could be vanquished by ignorance, fear and anxiety. Rome was simply unable to accept the truth. Power won. Evil held court. "I bowed my head reverently," he remembers, "in obedience to the spirit of the Church, the survival of Christ's Church, not because I feared the Pope." Ignorance made its force felt and darkness ruled Rome. The royal crown had become shabby. François is back again in olden times with his unsolved problems. He shakes himself out of his reverie and thinks: "That must now be over. Now my prayers, my devout prayers must be for the life of the soul with its new vision — not only for the Christ as I knew him. But can the Dark Brother bring redemption? Will I dare to speak the whole truth in the coming age without being punished by some vengeful authority?"

Kerel has observed François and registers his thoughts. Now he turns to him: "François, anything which does away with your roots is severing and would destroy the value of your experiences. Your 'friend,' Monsieur the Bishop of Meaux, whose bitter animosity tested you to the very core, and whose insidious ways almost succeeded in destroying you, was the very man you needed in order to reach the depths of your suffering and understanding."

Now Kerel, with his enigmatic smile, continues: "Did it ever occur to you, François, that the dark side of your soul can enter into a life which, knowing your foibles and weaknesses, will test your spirit of growth to the breaking point? That this Self-crucifixion can bring strength and rebirth? It is the way the Self tests earth existence to see if growth is still there, if the Tree of Life and Knowledge is still alive. François, you stayed alive in spirit; you did not stoop low but nobly went ahead. Bossuet's life accomplished its purpose to the full and, satisfied, the soul dropped it like an apple from a tree to let it rot away. Only the seeds will always live, to serve later on to test again the validity of life. I don't think that Bossuet will ever talk to you; he will be totally absorbed by you, François."

With a gracious bow and smile, François acknowledges Kerel's comment. He is impressed by his knowledge, but the moment of total acceptance has not yet come. So his courtly manner automatically comes to François' rescue. Nothing is settled in his mind yet, but Kerel has dropped a seed and knows that it will grow.

NEARER AND NEARER they come to Rome. They are all sad, infinitely sad and apprehensive — for what will happen to Rome? Now Wilfrid steps completely out of the mist and becomes clear. He loves Rome, for it is there that he found help and liberation in his lifetime. He wants to rush towards the Eternal City and touch the stones of Holy Church, but his feet refuse. He is torn apart, for Rome is not York or Canterbury; Rome is the center of the power he helped to establish in his homeland, and its rule was supreme. But the proud, eternal Center of the Apostolic succession has to meet its fate. "There is a time of glory, there is a time of sunrise, there is a time of sunset," he murmurs within himself. Now Wilfrid sees the cloud of York, Canterbury and Cambrai come closer and closer. He can't bear the sight. The relentless powers of the new Aeon are so gripping that again he tries to escape from them.

Spontaneously, a vision springs up in him of his Saint Peter's and the other churches he knew. He sees them, transparent, a ghostly memory of light and holiness — a memory of an all-prevailing universal truth, but without substance. The city becomes grey in his vision; it begins to rain. With the rain, the vision vanishes for ever. In this bewildered man of God, saint of the Holy Roman Church, only a memory of Rome's righteousness and fighting spirit remains.

François and Walter are not as perplexed as Wilfrid. They remember their disenchantment with Rome. They had expected truth and perspicacity to rule there, but, instead, they witnessed political manipulations. In spite of their priesthood, they now have a death wish for this holy city. So much evil, they feel, has been perpetrated in its sanctimonious atmosphere.

I see the three draw together, seeking protection in one another's nearness. They need one another, for at their feet lies the Holy City, the power, the glory of their Church which, they know, must meet its fate like all else in life. From their hilltop, they see the ever darkening sky gathering, leaving a strip of light on the horizon from where the setting sun is sending its last rays into the Eternal City. The windows, first reflecting like diamonds, become dull and then black holes. The stones and bricks are turning grey. "It is a town of clay," exclaims Walter. At that, the dark clouds emit their burden. The rain begins to pelt down-down-down — and down go the buildings as if the earth were absorbing its own. The Mother Church is received by the greater Mother Earth. Back again into the womb of darkness; as it was in the beginning, so it is in the end. To clay we return to be born again — but when? The Wheel of Life alone turns without end. All form shapes itself under its influence.

Kerel stoically stands watch over their psyche. François now weeps bitterly for the Rome which could not live up to his expectations. He feels the West was not able to produce enough men of noble spirit to set a lasting example for the rest of the world. Evil had to come and claim its power. Even the holy alchemy of the Church, he reflects, was not strong enough to stem the *Zeitgeist* of disintegration.

I think, unless the Dark wants to redeem itself, how can we ever live with the darkness of God's spirit?

Strong, rugged Walter, aware of François' deep religious feeling, turns to him and says: "My dear Fénelon, working with the Magna Carta, Parliament, the King and the Pope gave me a deep insight into worldly affairs. I see them as the temporary fruit of man's psychic history. I knew also that Rome could never bridge the worlds of the Crown and the Cross. In spite of this, my eyes were always on Rome. They should have been on Jerusalem, the roots of our spiritual heritage. That was my mistake."

Kerel knows full well that Rome had replaced Jerusalem. Neither François nor Wilfrid had ever realised that Walter also knew that. Wisdom comes from men who have handled the dark ways of life. The Black Mass which Walter once said to gain power over his youthful King has led him through the deepest darkness of suffering to the Light at the left hand of God.

Tighter and tighter they unite, needing one another's experience and holding on to the hope that in the blackness a degree of comprehension of the source of life can be found. Isn't that our quest?

Kerel is laden with the heavy heart of mankind as he begins to realize that the new spirit of the dual vision is, as yet, a total unknown — a cloud, a grey substance in which the light of pure spirit has disappeared.

Unwilling to enter Rome, the wayfarers travel around the city in a half circle towards the West and, in doing so, throw their shadows on Rome — once so great, so powerful, so corrupt, so worshipped. Only the light of the setting sun of a new day — mature, forgiving, full of warmth and understanding — can pay a fitting last tribute to the ruin that is Peter's Church.

Now I see them standing south of Rome: François, Walter, Wilfrid and Kerel and, further to the north, Christ and His Shadow-Brother. They know that Europe has to be left behind, but then, as one, they hesitate, they waver. Must they cross the Hellespont back to Asia? Must they leave Europe? Can't they go to Greece? Is Jerusalem so very important? Did the spirit of Greece not contribute brilliantly to the Christian mind? The West is their home, their love, and what might befall them if they cross over the waters to the cradle of Christianity? From the Middle East, their spirit had been catapulted to the wilds of a primitive Europe. They came to love Europe dearly, for it was there that they suffered their lives and built their churches — and their palaces also, although our bishops don't like this reminder of their elegant, worldly ways. They all thought they were so spiritual — except for Walter, who was fully aware of the cost of stately living and the price he paid for it. Such thoughts are the best antidote for that personal halo which Wilfrid and François still have wobbling slightly around their heads.

Kerel stands as irresolute as his companions. He knows that he will be forced to become conscious of a deeper level of his Universal Self. He is about to enter the Near East. To cross the Hellespont means that he will return to the cradle of Christianity, nearer the magic battlefield of Arjuna, where Yahweh ruled when Christ was born. That was the time when the power of the Logos faced the newly budding Eros: the majesty of creation facing the flower of Love incarnate in frail humankind. An aeon of suffering has passed. What will the future bring? Kerel feels burdened, bruised and near melancholy, for where is the light of the future?

August 10
Sils Maria

I KNOW WHY they hesitate and philosophize: there is an emotional block in their psyches, something not yet experienced which belongs to their pilgrimage. When they circled Rome, following the shape of the crescent moon, they made a night's journey in which much was left undigested. The farewell to the Eternal City was too painful to bear. Fear had plugged their ears; their noses had omitted the smells. They just *saw* the debacle.

Rome had cried out to them: "Save us! Save the churches of Peter and Paul!" Why Peter and Paul? Why not in the name of Christ? Rome's grey pleading voices had lost their luster. Peter and Paul are history — only the Christ is eternal.

Now, as they look back on the city, a rain of ashes and dust descends. Once it was the hope of mankind; now it is only the agony. Kerel, touched to the core, just stands and watches. The full realization of the debacle is upon them. François weeps convulsively over the lost opportunities for greatness. Walter stands silent, numb, while tears stream down his grooved face. Wilfrid, his hands lifted, begins to hum a beloved Gregorian chant which he composed with his singer Willibald during their pilgrimage to the Holy City. He sings firmly now and, with that alchemy, digests the pain of destruction. With each stanza, Rome sinks deeper into his heart. It is not there, out on the bleak landscape, but safely tucked away in his chest, and deeper still is his Jerusalem. What he once experienced of Rome's beauty, spirituality and strength, and carried so happily back to Ripon and York, will not be lost; neither will the Church's efforts to recreate the Kingdom of Heaven on earth. It is all well stored within Wilfrid, and so he is the first to turn his back on the ashes and walk ahead towards his future.

The others have to stand there for a while: they are thinking. If Rome has not provided the living truth they seek, might not Jerusalem also turn their hopes into dust? Can this earth support the Heavenly Kingdom? They look at Wilfrid, going ahead with a sturdy stride; there is even a glow, an aura around his lithe body. Kerel recalls the leading spirit that is ever a part of Wilfrid and can't suppress his amusement. That priestly rascal always barges ahead once his goal is set. The others follow, for haven't they always pursued that which is numinous? They call to him and he stops, glad to have his companions join him.

"Wait, Wilfrid, where are you going?" they ask.

"To Jerusalem, of course," he answers.

"You seem to be full of portent; purpose radiates from you."

With a majestic sweep of the arm, he motions to his spirit brothers to follow him. "Come with me to Jerusalem," he shouts, "as we still must see what It may reveal to us, or what we can accomplish there." Kerel is delighted with the new mood created by this old fighter, but he is also somewhat dubious about what still lies ahead.

Before Jerusalem can be reached, there is still one more spirit brother to be visited: Asterius, Archbishop of Amasia. The Near East is much alive in Wilfrid's memory. Amasia is remembered in his Eternal Mind, and he is strongly attracted to that city. He doesn't intuit at all, however, what gruesome initiations are in store. Neither François, nor Walter, nor Kerel, for that matter, has any idea of the immense change to come which, unknowingly, they are helping to bring about.

On they go; a pioneering spirit is affecting their blood. The unseen power behind them influences every step of the way. They cannot act differently; they are caught in the vise-like grip of the new era and moved to cross the waters toward the native land of their soul.

My emotions are in upheaval. I admire my ancestral components: their spell is on me. I feel every one of them and, at times, I am torn apart. Then, again, my apprehensions are completely overridden by an inner surge of confidence. My inner being watches my progress and I write and write. Its voice, impossible to override, is dictating to me.

The spirit of Light and Darkness, the spirit of Christ and Satanic Lucifer which has followed them from Northern France, is slowly spreading all over the world. If they had looked back, our wayfarers, if their eyes were not directed, so full of hope, towards Amasia and Jerusalem, they WOULD have seen what Kerel knew was happening: a world in conflagration and turmoil, a miraculous merging of the numinous and nigredo meant not to destroy the past, nor to prevent the future, but to create, with terror-striking power, of being, a world in which the mighty as well as the meek spirits will seek expression to establish the next human kingdom on this Heavenly earth.

IN AMASIA, on the other side of the Hellespont, Asterius, totally unaware of any change to come, is laughing, for they are all coming back home. He is a stocky, strong man and he laughs heartily and long. He will give them a wonderful welcome, and they will hear about another Christianity which he lived. No Rome nor wicked Constantinople could ever dampen his spirit, not even after Eusebius sent persecutors to try to kill him. They left him for dead by the roadside with a broken hip. Limping and undaunted, he preached in a deep voice the apostolic message according to his innate nature and his experience of the Christ Jesus within him. For almost a hundred years, he had lived that life and, with golden tongue, declared the wonders of Christ. It was a time rampant with the evil power drives of an emerging theology. But always with him are the memories of masses of people, searching for the deep experiences and ecstasies of saintly men to lift themselves out of dark primitivity into Christ-like awareness. Indeed, he fills the fourth century church of Amasia with the greatness of his vibrant personality.

I now see our wayfarers nearing Amasia, tiny figures moving on and on. I see the momentum, the roads, and, as in real life I wonder how I can travel so far, so constantly over this globe, as if in traveling I will fulfill my quest and find an answer to the question which has changed with every milestone I have reached.

Our wayfarers now reach Amasia. With his usual passionate vitality and warmth, Asterius has prepared a wonderful welcome for his friends. Astute, worldly, yet deeply religious in the purest sense, he is like a rock of strength and confidence. He never changes; no age seems to affect him. He is still in the fourth century, undaunted as ever, and completely unaware of the cosmic Now in which his soul mates travel.

In full regalia of cloth of gold, Asterius stands alone, waiting on the steps in front of the portal to the shrine of his beloved Christ. There are no crowds, there is no music, all is blue-grey. All alone, he stands there, solemn in the full majesty of his office. The entourage to which he is so accustomed is not with him. He is imbued with the powers of the Apostolic blessing and again experiences the curious mingling of Lord and servant.

He sways slightly, shakes his head, juts out his square jaw, and looks piercingly with his dark eyes into the blue-grey of his surroundings. He pushes his long hair behind his ears and wriggles inside his stocky body. Is he asleep or dreaming? His aloneness is in such contrast to the time when he stood on the very same spot — years ago — waiting to receive the bones of Saint Phocas, the first martyr to have his remains, "the tabernacle of his holy mind," installed in the Lord's shrine. Asterius is filled with a warm glow of satisfaction: he is the one who initiated the rites for the adoration and glorification of this simple martyr. "That was then," he thinks, "but what now? Am I dreaming? Asleep or awakening from my eternal slumber? How strange, this blue-grey light."

He wants to walk but cannot. His feet seem rooted in the cathedral steps. He lifts his shorter left leg; yes, it can move. He lifts his right one; yes, it moves also. But he cannot walk. "Travel within," says his inner voice, "travel deeper and realize how your progeny, Wilfrid, became Saint of York. Remember the agonies of your soul during those barbaric days in the West. Primitive England! It made you withdraw and go back to sleep; later, you wanted to interfere in that life and force Wilfrid to stay in Rome."

"Memories of the past, flee from me! Don't haunt me with what I couldn't accomplish. Soothe me with my achievements, the great sermons, the power I had to sway the masses to adore the Lord and see His Glory!"

"No," says the inner voice, "that is all gone and done — done well, but your soul has moved on, anxious to live and perform what could not be achieved in your century. Your fourth century, like any other time, allowed just so much and accomplished only its limited tasks. Awake and await that which you did not live. Fear not. Flash your beautiful smile and look with your dark eyes on the unfolding of your soul life. See what your Self has had to experience through the centuries. The end of time is nearing. You have to know what could not be done in your Piscean Age."

"Again a call to life?" Asterius asks himself.

"Life is unending," retorts his inner voice, "no rest ever, only change from what is and was in order to experience the everlasting variety of man's expressions."

How well he knows that voice. "No wonder," he thinks, "that, five centuries after I spoke, that very same voice was so eagerly sought after in my homilies. Who knows, perhaps that is the everlasting Presence, the Unknown Divine in my soul and mind. That voice in its greatest moment spoke through Jesus." He trembles because he has experienced its emotional power so often. Tears well up, he feels a tremor in his heart like a far-off thunder — or is it perhaps the rumbling of an earthquate? It is the moment of confrontation with the unfolding of his life work and what his Center has had to experience through the centuries.

Looking down the street leading to the cathedral square, he now observes the slow approach of his expected guests. Four tired travelers they are. There is something remarkable and strange about them. Is he truly the ancestor of these men? In Kerel, he sees the glow of the Eternal Light, Wilfrid reflects the Holy spirit of Rome, Walter is like the brown earthly riches of power, and in Fénelon Asterius sees an elegance of bearing and culture that are so close to him. He notices that the stars of each of his further incarnations are shining over their heads through the dark shadows and strange lights of their auras. These are not just men — they are peculiar saints, or men imbued by a new Light unknown to him. Apprehensive now, he steps back towards the portal of his stronghold. Suddenly the building is filled with thunderous music, and he hears drums beating in strange rhythms, shrill piping, and a heavenly choir of voices singing unknown stanzas. The darkness around the heavenly aura of the four pilgrims becomes more intense now, and fierce lightning pierces the heavens. It seems as if they may be struck at any moment, but this possibility does not even occur to them.

This greatly anticipated welcome, this high moment of encounter and reunion becomes a frightening, terror-striking event to Asterius. He throws up his arms to the heavens, only to hear derisive laughter followed by the thunderous belch of the Gods. Hurriedly, urgently, he makes the sign of the cross in the direction of the men, who seem to unleash unknown forces all around them. They are so few in number, yet so powerful in portent.

Now I feel myself shaking with Asterius, I feel his impulses. His very being is in me, alive, potent. Nothing is asleep, all is awareness. There is a total resurrection of my ancient spirit. My twentieth century being is one with the past. Time is not: I am experiencing another life; another awareness is absorbed and, shaking with excitement, I write; but I am not just the recorder, I am playing my role fully — past and present.

Then I hear a loud, the loudest possible crash of thunder following the very moment where Kerel puts his left foot on the first step of the cathedral, this shrine of Christ. At that instant, the world of Asterius is broken.

> Wonder of Wonders!
> Miracle of Miracles!
> Holy of Holiest Moments in Time!

Another step has been fulfilled. With Kerel, the flow of wisdom from the East, transformed and vitalized by the spiritual experiences of the West, reenters the East. The Ouroboros is complete.

A Change in the Unchangeable!

No one knows what will be brought about next. Strong, Christ-loving Asterius is on his knees. The overwhelming forces of nature joined with the presence of the four culminate now in a strange and unheard-of spectacle. Out of the church stalks a lion rampant with seven tails and five heads in one. Grabbing Asterius by the shoulders from behind, the Lion raises him off his feet with magic ease and penetrates this saint of the early church with his fiery, life-giving rod. It is a shocking manifestation like those in *Revelations*.

Totally overwhelmed, Asterius leans against his assailant for support. Oh Lord, what next will be demanded of this sturdy soul? The four companions, although they have experienced so much, are in awe of this spectacle. Is this to happen to them? Is this the way to Jerusalem? While they watch and wonder, they see the great majestic Lion turn his prey around to confront the church. Large cracks begin to appear on both sides of the holy edifice, then walls split apart as if they were struck by lightning. Clouds of rose-mauve dust rise all about them, giving the impression of sunset although the sun has barely risen.

Released from the intimate embrace, Asterius is pushed magically into the church toward the altar. Unable to walk, he senses himself floating and freed of the pain in his left thigh which, ever since his torture, has always been part of him. His visitors follow, accustomed by now to broken arches and stones strewn about like pebbles on the beach.

Kerel is deeply impressed by the events. Sensitive François, too much identified with Asterius, is numb and holds his buttocks as if he were the one who had been violated. Walter feels, curiously enough, as if he could understand this symbolic rite, and memories of his black masses well up again. Wilfrid is bewildered, for the faint memory he has of the East, through his former lives, cannot find any echo in this spectacle. But none of them, none of them can remotely evaluate the event.

They are carried along in this terrifying drama of Birth and Rebirth, Death and Life, Darkness and Light. They are all held in the power of the newly emerging God and his enlarged concept of the wholeness of life — not just the spirit of the Father, but that of the Earth-Mother as well; not just one serpent as Redeemer but two serpents, entwined in an eternal Ecstasy of Being; not just the contortions of the One, but the steady rhythms of the Two. This is the uniting of all that was split apart when Lightning rent the veil of the Temple at the time of the Crucifixion. The descent of the Lord is imminent; the Marriage is approaching its fulfillment.

Asterius, followed by the four travelers, moves down the middle aisle. They mount the steps toward the main altar. How many times has the Holy Ghost descended there at that altar into the celebrant of the mass, who, being so imbued, in turn blessed the congregation. This ageless ritual, so familiar to our little group, has been their strength and is the backbone of their spiritual being.

With Kerel in the middle, they form a semicircle in front of the holy place. In anguish, they watch the miraculous disappearance of the altar; instead of the ancient sacrificial table, the Pit of Darkness is revealed, reaching beyond the crypt and into the land of the dead and the damned.

There they see the unlived, the unwanted, that which could not be except in the hopes of mankind, shattered fragments of human attempts, and their willful tragedies. Deeper down the Pit reaches, into all and everything that can be suffered and redeemed by our human psyches. Below that, and beyond reach of any human, lies the unbearable suffering of God for his human race. That is the mysterious dark layer called primordial life which boils up in great bubbles at times with the unmistakable purpose of becoming humanoid, and of starting on the road into human consciousness, where its black pitch must find a way into the suffering awareness leading to its redemption.

How long a road, thinks Kerel, how endless a task! Can we stay alive long enough as a race to suffer that misery? Can my human brain comprehend this road of evolution? He looks at the archbishops, who simply stare, perplexed.

While priests and congregation were receiving the blessings of the one-sided Light of Christ, all that which did not belong to that spiritual kingdom had gone unattended. Spirit, regarded as eternally triumphant, was supreme, and earth cried out in vain. The nether regions were left doomed, locked up, shackled as black pestilence, awaiting the time mankind would be developed enough to comprehend the divinity of All — the Black and the White, the Darkness and the Light — all His creation, for All is sacred in its own way.

As our pilgrims look into the Pit of Eternal Darkness, a lamenting howl softly rises and chills their bones. Raising their hands and eyes for a prayer of mercy, they slowly become aware through the stench, dust, and vapors of the atmosphere that two hands are forming opposite the Pit, full of grace and beauty, unutterably precious and strong. With infinite tenderness, the Left and Right Hands of God move toward each other to unite, and out of this union a ladder is formed, descending deep into the Black. From above, large bitter tears of blood and sorrow begin to fall into the Pit — God's tears shed for man, to resurrect and enliven all that was buried of the human race. Winds of prayer, culminating in a storm, now encircle this divine Pit, as it is not without fear that God encounters his own creation.

"O ye around the Pit,"

God thunders, even though he tries to whisper in order not to destroy with His immensity,

"Ye around this Pit of the Unlived,
  Bow your head and pray with Me,
    For here is our fulfillment.
      Out of this womb will rise all

That is within you
　　　　As you are conceived in My image.
"In My ignorance I brought you here. Out of ignorance you came here yourselves.

"Receive all this darkness and what it may contain for each of you as My blessing.

"Pray and work for the development of your soul, your soul being the only living creation through which I perceive knowledge of My own Being.

"Bend your knees and know that your divinity is dependant upon your being human.

"Neither plant nor animal can encroach upon Me but through your being. For you are my channel to awareness and greater consciousness of all that is on earth as formed by Me and Me alone."

The village clock of Sils strikes; it is high noon.

Now God's Voice descends to the music of everyday language, all the more devastating and penetrating because of its utter simplicity and matter-of-factness.

"The new day is dawning. Through Me the Christ will be reborn. My only begotten Son will travel into the Greater Light containing the deeper strata of Life's Darkness. And you — Kerel, François, Walter, Wilfrid, Asterius — you are My channel; the development of Christ's church in you is now complete. The time of the Fishes is over. I send you the Waterman, inexperienced but full of new powers and archaic wisdom. Go on your journey to Jerusalem, and see what revelations will come your way. But do not tarry; humanity is waiting."

August 13
Sils Maria

Humanity can wait.

THERE THEY SIT on the bank beside the road to Jerusalem; now they are five. How can they travel? So burdened, so heavily burdened! This revelation is hardly to their liking. It is far too unsettling.

Asterius, once so sure of his faith, so eager to welcome his friends, so ready to help them unburden themselves, sits there, perplexed and indignant. The rape has affected him almost more than the revelation of the Pit of Hell and of Unlived Life. His buttocks are sore and his intestines smart from the hot, lava-like substance spurted into him.... "Lord Jesus, what a foul awakening," he thinks. "Is this the spirit of the Pit, this creature from the Bible's *Revelations*? Is it actually alive?" Outraged and furious, he wants to shout, "Revenge, revenge!" But, at that moment, voices of a heavenly choir singing "Hallelujah" intercede and drown out these thoughts. He shakes his head violently and now his body even reacts with delight, and a secret pleasure is in his bowels. What a thing to accept! Then, to his amazement, he has the feeling that he carries the long horn of the Unicorn on his forehead, and his skull tingles slightly at the place where the root would be. He feels his head. Thank God, there is nothing there.

Asterius looks at his companions but meets only Kerel's laughing eyes and a nod which shows he is fully aware of the archbishop's thoughts. A shrug of Asterius' shoulders is the only response. But Kerel, with his ancient mind, knows that the law of opposites is at work. No new Aeon of Aquarius will change that. The Unicorn, a symbol of Christ and His strength, is there at the same time as is the pleasurable feeling in the bowels. Perhaps the New Age will bring a better relationship between the opposites, muses Kerel, thinking of the ladder leading down into the Pit.

Asterius' mind travels back to his Amasia. He stands up to look at his ancient town. It is still there, and he thinks he can perceive the large roof of his church, but not the tower. Is this a trick of his imagination? Will he ever accept the complete debacle and disappearance of his church? He is unable to imagine, as yet, that the landscape is not dominated by his cathedral — all these events are too overwhelming for him. Then, suddenly, his thoughts are pulled back to his belly. What devils and dragons have been created in him, he wonders? He sits down with a loud noise — and that settles that, for the smell is like the breath of the devil. Asterius is undone.

François, always fastidious, looks up amazed at Asterius' lack of manners. With a sigh, he accepts, for isn't this just a minor disturbance? Perhaps his spirit has to become more acquainted with the impact of the opening of the Pit below the altar. "My esthetic being is really my stumbling block," François thinks. "Are the vulgarities of life to be taken less seriously? But what will happen to the delights and grandeur of life? They are so important, for they create an atmosphere in which my spirit can live. What attitude do I take toward that Pit of Hell? Should I be gracious to a pestilent thought? Shall I allow myself to look the monster in the eye and reason with him or it — instead of kicking it back into hell?"

François' entire system seems to be drained; no answer rises up. "Lord knows I have dealt with evil in men and women. How did I ever escape from being devoured by my enemies? I know I created them by being frank and open and as truthful as possible. But truth doesn't always hold wisdom, and it is better silenced so that my tongue won't be cut out."

Bitter worldly thoughts, thoughts of the Pit. François becomes aware that it holds perhaps a great part of his being, and the heavy sadness of silence in his soul weighs him down. Deeper he goes now into those memories of his being which were not allowed to take form or be expressed in words, and created in him a heart so burdened that the simple shock of a carriage accident brought him to his prayerful death. Searching for the soothing comfort of Holy Scripture, he had escaped from the pain of his being. Indeed he knows now that he has a Pit in himself.

"What else will be brought up that I haven't already met?", he asked himself. "I remember writing once near my end: 'I think I have no desire to taste of the world. It seems as if there is a barrier between it and me, which prevents any longing on my part and which would, I fancy, stand not a little in my way were I, one day, called upon to return to it.' "

Walter and Wilfrid are holding hands; no, Walter's hand is resting on Wilfrid's. The two men from York know much about the Pit and shudder at the thought of having to deal with all that devilish black part of life again.

After a while, Walter gets up and moves away from his companions. He looks at the other side of the bank. There, behind a dry moat, rises a wall with a single window. Is it a castle? In the window sits the nubile maiden Miriam. She sits and spins and sings an endless song to hide the pain within. It is not a lament — it is the song of Not Knowing what is or has been.

Walter looks up at her, waves and is noticed. Smilingly, she waves back and puts her spindle aside. She smiles in her own way the smile of a woman who has suffered beyond endurance, longer than can be known. One who is made to suffer, she is — and because of that incredibly beautiful to man's soul. She leans out of the window: "I might perhaps come down to you, men, for I know your fate and I know you as harbingers of freedom of spirit."

Walter raises his eyebrows in surprise and smiles at this turn of events. He answers: "Soul travelers, we are, in search of Jerusalem, the City of the Golden Heart." What makes me say that?, he wonders.

"I know. I know you are right. Christ is waiting.

The City of God will open its gate wide, but it will not be the way you expect it. Tarry a while and I will join you, from beyond this moat separating Life from Death. I too will be on my way. I have been sitting here an aeon — waiting-waiting-waiting endlessly, waiting for the end of time. Don't be upset if I cry as I appear: it will be from happiness as well as grief, the same pain we all experience at every birth." She disappears, throwing a kiss to Walter.

Have the others seen this? Yes, Kerel has, of course; the others were all too preoccupied with their own thoughts and the black hole under and beyond the altar of Christianity.

Here she comes, clutching her skirts to free the path for her feet. Both hands hold up the coarsely woven material. She goes straight to Walter, makes her little curtsy and says calmly: "Don't worry, only Kerel and you can see me. Like you, I have come a long way, but my way through the ages was one of observing — no acting, only painfully observing the fate of the mute women, the God-bearing pregnant women. Part of God is in all men. I have always known that I am not the only God-bearing woman. I am Miriam, the Virgin. Isha Jahu had me in mind when, seven centuries before, he prophesied the birth of Emmanuel. He is my son. In Isha's being I was formed; his spirit carried silently the immensity of the suffering woman-spirit in humanity. It is because of him that I survived. It is because of him that there was comfort at all."

With eyes almost glazed, she continues: "I heard time and time again, 'Comfort ye, comfort ye!' The Lord of Hosts in his mightiness eyes the sufferer as his jewel; then I would have peace, until the spasms of agony in human existence convulsed my wretched woman's soul. Oh, how I would echo painfully to the heart-strings of my true being."

"The Divine, having foreseen and foretold the muting of women's voice, enthroned me as a symbol of divine virtue without ever giving me the chance to speak or commune. I am the symbol of silent Death; the howling note of cosmic suffering is heard in my heart. I carry the cosmic pain, that is why all people come to me, for silent understanding and mute strength. In my frail unformed body I formed the body of the Man Who carried out the spoken message and Who enacted the divine drama with His disciples. But I was mute, my song not heard, so, in the subterranean passages of life, as if in a maze, I moved unheard. Some of the church builders knew it in their hearts, and pictured my path on their church floors where, like me, men and women would crawl on their knees through the maze for absolution and to pacify their grief. But unnoticed, silently, my spirit crept all over the world. Kwan Yin — Maria — whatever name was given me represents the feminine mercy of God's Being."

Miriam sighs now and smiles again, but much more brightly. "The spirit of the comforter is returning, Walter, with you and your friends. He will know about my new road and, like a cosmic pawn, the stars will move me to my new bridegroom. When He is ready, He will again open my womb but, this time, also my lips. What will escape, what will be first, the Lord only knows, but I will have a voice. My belly rumbles already and the earth is agitated, and now I am shaking — SHAKING, do you hear?" She shouts "shaking" and emits a fearful belch which awakens every one of our travelers out of his reverie. No one sees her, for she is swallowed up by the tree, against which she had put her hand to steady her shaking, shaken self. But now the earth shakes and shakes and ripples the countryside.

"The Virgin's healing breasts," cries Kerel, all of a sudden.

"No, her God-bearing belly," answers Walter, and the others, simply bewildered by these explosive words, watch as the road moves like the waves of an ocean. And the rounding movement of the earth is as the breasts and belly of the Virgin, and everywhere there is a fragrance as of orchids, and the love for God is like an explosive dynamism in the soul of the travelers, for now they are all standing and being moved toward their goal; they gasp for air, and each gasp is like the wine of life as they come nearer the seat of their soul. Divinely drunk, they stare ahead as the undulating earth directs them towards Jerusalem. The road moves them as if they were floating on an ocean's groundswell. Jerusalem is not drawing them so much as the earth is pushing them toward the City.

Behind their backs, the tree brings forth Miriam again, and she joins with the unseen but ever-present rear guard. The Prince of Light and the Prince of Darkness have been slowly walking their straight path toward Jerusalem. They, too, go toward their destiny and will wait in the garden of the Holy Temple until they are called to enter. They go slowly, for Miriam's spirit is like lead. Two thousand years of pain are carried by the adolescent woman. The Virginal Maiden wonders about so many things as she leans heavily on her companions. At times, her knees buckle. She is now at the end of her road. A few more steps and she will find relief. "Can I make it, now that relief is in sight?" She does not seem to care at this moment. "Forward, forward," she hears from somewhere. Her legs move, her hands press on her heart. The load is too heavy. All humanity's wounded love is upon her. "Like an Atlas, I have to be", she exclaims, and stops. "I can't collapse now. Where will I find the strength to go on?"

A cry of agonized surprise makes her look up. The wayfarers have reached their goal, and, oh my God, it is not Jerusalem, but the square beak of an enormous monster which is about to swallow them up. The agony in Wilfrid's backward glance helps Miriam. He throws out his right arm in a plea, for they are entering the beak of the monster. It is the plea for help which gives her life, strength. So, with her smile of beatitude, she waves back and automatically fulfills her eternal role of Man's support in distress. But this time, she knows that it is not a son calling on her, but a man, a mature, warm-hearted man, who knows suffering, and it awakens in her the woman-mate, the companion, the cotraveler in the cosmic maze.

Then, with an enormous throaty gurgle, the

monster passes our pilgrims through the gateway beak right into the center of Jerusalem.

After thousands of years of human effort and struggle with divine destiny, the City of God, the new Jerusalem, has come to Earth. The promised land is now open to all, even unto Moses.

Jerusalem! Cool air, magnificent atmosphere, crystal clearness all around, our wayfarers stand awed, overwhelmed by the immensity of the love of God surging through them. It is as if an electric shock had stunned them. Soon, however, rather too soon, the five travelers recover their senses. The critical mind, with all the limitations it suffers when confronted with the unknown, begins to work in François. With French disdain, he says: "Eh bien, this does not mean anything. Somewhere there will be foul play." Walter is pleased, relieved perhaps to have a short breathing space, while Wilfrid swallows the whole experience with delight. Asterius says with great feeling: "Bah, we will be fooled again," but he is glad of the respite. Kerel simply observes the beautiful marketplace, hub of all spirituality, and now completely empty except for our wayfarers. All is obsolutely quiet, as if humanity had deserted the City of Redemption.

The silence is broken by a rhythmic tapping. Our pilgrims turn and see a beggar with a cane coming toward them from a side street. Kerel knows him; the others recall him faintly. Yes, he is one of them: their first Christian ancestor, Judas Barsabas, son of a wealthy tentmaker of the tribe of Judah and a prophet in his own right. Schooled and trained in the Greek tradition, he is a highly civilized man who helped Paul and Silas bring the teachings of Jesus, the Christ, to the gentiles of Antioch. Judas is bent and tired today because, in spite of his convictions, a restless mental activity forces him to probe constantly into the mysteries of life.

"You're all back," he says, "in this glorious town in which I am a beggar." He looks at all his descendants: so there they are, they have come home. He welcomes them all. The travelers are now quick to recognize him and encircle him warmly, feeling their affiliation with this quizzical-looking man. They stare intensely at him and he at them without speaking a word. Only the eyes are communicating, and, through this curious language, springs a greater awareness. They sense that they are all one, and that Judas is the original Christian in their family.

Barsabas is proud of what has developed out of his soul: priests and wise men. He knows this could have happened only on account of that one moment of full comprehension he experienced when he visited the field of Golgotha where Christ was crucified. Barsabas' spirit wants to travel back to the great events of the past, but this is not the time for it. So, gathering himself to face the present moment, he says with a slightly mysterious smile: "My wife knows that you are here and has sent me to welcome you. She is All that is, both Witch and Angel, and even God mirrors himself in Her. I wonder in what state she will receive you."

As Judas turns to lead his guests toward his crystal house situated right in front of them on the square, a terrific gust of wind whips away the curtain in front of the entrance and reveals a beautiful warm hall with red carpets — a lovely welcome to the fatigued travelers. Judas invites them all in: "This is my wife's home, where I live most of the time," he says. "She sends her love and will see you when you are refreshed, bathed, and ready for dinner."

At long last the wayfarers have arrived. This is their house, their home. Overwhelmed and exhausted, they enter.

August 14
Sils Maria

"WHY ARE YOU a beggar?" asks Wilfrid, when they are refreshed and reunited in the Hall.

"This life is my doom as well as my reward," answers Judas. "For I am always too mental, not accepting life as it is. Through begging I learn to take what is given me and to live accordingly. When I rebel, I go hungry, and my misery leads me to acceptance once again. When I accept my state of mind, whatever it is, I am provided for, and then I automatically return to this house which is my home. But I do rebel, and I doubt. But that too is a blessing, for then I learn and often get to know more than my wife who sits here in her eternal bliss." Judas thinks of his sweet Sophia and smiles. His wife is a very complicated lady. "She knows that my rebellion is also a pilgrimage, and that my experience adds to her wisdom, although she hates to admit it and becomes a real she-devil when I tell her a few home truths which she doesn't know yet. Being married to a Goddess, a High Priestess, is sheer hell for my human side, but bliss in the time between my pilgrimages. And so we are united with the strongest ties."

Then he silences his tongue. "What now?" he wonders. "What will I do? Do they know that Sophia is also God's wife? Will they be upset knowing I am married to God in a tripartite? How will Sophia welcome them? What aspect of the Wisdom of God will she reveal?"

There is no smile left on Judas' lips now that

the moment of confrontation has arrived. It is as if a black hand gently grips his golden heart as he senses that the purpose of the long trek from York to Jerusalem nears its climax.

Suddenly a blast of heavenly trumpets sounds and blends into one note, transforming Judas into a divine pawn who majestically turns around to lead the way to the north wall of the Hall. A round door appears and opens slowly. Our pilgrims follow Judas in single file through this "Breathing Hole of Eternity." It is a solemn procession and each of them feels the momentous occasion.

Now they are six — six, the number of blackness and dynamic power, but also the human expression of the Trinity. So they enter. "Oh, God, what now?" A fearful shudder goes through them. Their skin prickles; their backbones tingle as they experience the atmosphere of this most holy room. What they see is a simple setting for an evening supper, arranged on a plain table. Some see a cloth, others a cleanly scrubbed surface.

But who is seated there? It is not a woman, not a man. Facing them is the very spirit of an immense Idea, the stark simplicity of the Christ in its most awesome form. Is this Judas' wife? There is light all around in that mysterious fashion one experiences in dreams. They all realize and know that this will be their Last Supper. Two thousand years have passed, and now at the end of time it is as at the beginning. Then, the Piscean myth descended to earth; only now can they experience the myth in its totality, thus rounding out the old and starting the new in the psyche of all mankind. Deep down in their being, the six recognize that they are descendants also of Peter and Paul, and they look for their friends — John, Matthew, Mark and Thomas — with whom they shared their experiences. Is Stephen far away? And Andros, where is he? They all seem to be there, but unseen.

The Man of Light rises calmly, and Judas introduces each of the wayfarers by his first name. The Man nods and says: "You seem familiar to me. In fact, I remember most of what you did in your lifetimes." Then he sits down, motioning to his guests to do likewise. As they are being seated by Judas, the light of Christ's face changes and becomes warm and human.

"I am Jesus of Nazareth," he says simply, breaking the bread and pouring the wine. He looks at the men kindly and drinks. All raise their glasses and some tears drop into the wine. Walter chokes and part of his wine spills out of his mouth onto the table.

"Bless you, Walter, you choke on your Black Mass, don't you?" Jesus asks.

The shock of drinking with Christ Jesus is too much for Walter. And so he reacts in a most primitive and vicious manner.

"No. On you. Who do you say you are?"

"Jesus of Nazareth," is the calm answer.

"Where is the Christ?" Walter asks brusquely, shocking the others.

"In you and me," He answers.

"Sure, sure, I know. And His Shadow?" Walter persists.

"In you and me," comes the reply.

"You are damned right," says Walter. "In me and in you." He looks ahead, staring into space, remembering the endless suffering he has undergone at his own death and the acceptance of his duality and all that is in him. He hears bells ring and toll.

At this very moment, in actuality, I hear the bells start to ring here in Sils Maria on this Sunday morning.

An aeon of suffering sweeps through Walter which gives him strange strength. He stands up calmly, walks from his bench toward Jesus and puts his arms around him. They kiss and embrace.

The others do not understand what is happening. They do not comprehend that this is Walter's moment of complete acceptance of his Black Mass. He has suffered it, and so has Jesus. This mutual experience has broken the spell of awe in Walter. He recognises that Jesus is not the Christ of two thousand years ago, but that unbelievably mature, wise man who has realised what has happened in the last aeon. Walter senses you can be intimate with this man, you can love his warmth as long as you remain connected with your own warmth and do not cheat your human side.

Then Jesus turns to Walter and says: "Look!" He shows him two fangs protruding from his mouth. Walter takes one fang in his hand, shakes it slightly and says with a sigh and so sadly: "Yes, do I know! Yes, indeed." He then shows his own menacing teeth. Walter's hand now clasps the hand of Jesus the Christ and thus they sit sadly together for a while. A deep tie of mutual and painful experience seems to forge them together. There is no difference at this moment between Christ Jesus and Christ Walter.

"What can develop now?" Judas wonders, watching them all. Kerel, with head in hand, is toying with the bread and turning his wine glass. François doesn't understand the bond between Walter and Jesus. He hears the strains of a music incomprehensible to him as yet, a cadence totally foreign to his seventeenth-century ear. It chills his bones and, to warm himself, he gathers his train around his feet. They are freezing. He realises how far he has journeyed from his stately Court into the present setting of timeless simplicity. Closing his eyes, he prays fervently to the Almighty for comfort and understanding.

Wilfrid looks astonished, only faintly comprehending the new alliance between Jesus and Walter. With his right hand, he reaches for Asterius' comforting presence, but Asterius is only half there. He is deeply withdrawn and in a state of shock brought on by the relentless assault of devastating events with which he has had to cope. Judas, much worried, sees Asterius float away in a cloud of despair. Trying to get him back, Judas sends him all his love and affection, but apparently Asterius can return only when he becomes willing to weep uncontrollably. He is floating back into the front hall to grasp the one pillar that is there; and then, without a sob or a sound, the tears start to pour. He is so sad, so terribly upset. He had seen the protruding fangs in both men, and that mutual recognition which seems so important to Walter and Jesus is just hideous to him. Judas, who has gone begging so many times, excuses himself from the table and goes to the hall to console Asterius and bring him back into his own. He puts his arm around the shocked Bishop of Amasia and walks back and forth with him in front of the unlit hearth.

"Beloved brother, don't try to hold back your sobs. To see the duality of Jesus Christ is frightening. At first, I saw only His Shadow and had trouble seeing His Light. I knew Jesus before the days he was the Christ, and I didn't really accept His mission until I experienced what happened at the Cross, the terrible marriage between the human-animal or animal-human side and the presence of God, a moment of death, oblivion and tearing apart — a rending departure into the heavens of God's spirit which has walked the earth, and a new spiritual union between God and Man prevailed."

Judas sighs as he contemplates whether he should continue to relate his experiences. The need of the moment decides, thus he continues: "I didn't follow all the teachings of Jesus, and especially not those of His disciples. I did experience, however, that dreadfully important moment when God is Christ, Jesus and Man, all united in an embrace so that nothing more exists but their power inalienably together, forever. Something happened, not just there on the hill of Golgotha, but everywhere in the cosmos. At the instant of that union, activated by the Holy Ghost, a reality became available to all mankind."

Asterius only nods; he needs to hear a sympathetic voice. "Just talk, just talk to me, Judas," he pleads. Judas is only too glad to continue; he senses that he has never spoken so fully from his heart.

"Registering this divine drama was most difficult for me and nearly cost me my life. For years after that experience, I was frail. The marrow of my bones was almost burned out by the searing fire of God's presence. It is only in that burning supreme moment that there is Absolute Union." He pauses and continues." "Later on, many have suffered similar experiences, and Walter came close to it at his death. A priceless gift was waiting for him. He was old and tired from his work, and his ego was no longer dominant. Only then was he prepared to enter into a union with his Self. On his death-bed, he could suffer the pain of his power-drunk blackness which, to his astonishment, brought about a clear vision and contact with his innermost being. Through his suffering, he recognised an aspect of the Light in his own darkness. He never forgot this. The revelation of the evil fangs shows the hard road we have to travel to come to a fuller comprehension of our duality. This is the basis of the understanding that exists between Jesus and Walter."

Asterius senses the warmth of Judas' feeling which is so reassuring, but he finds it hard to accept the idea that Light can be reached through the darkness of evil. He can only vaguely compare the suffering of Walter with that of the redeemed thief on the cross. His heart reacts, for he feels that Judas speaks with love and true wisdom, the wisdom of personal experience — an idea lived, not just comprehended. "The Inner Light comes from the experience suffered," Judas adds.

Judas' revelatory account and the love that has brought it about pull like a magnet and bring Jesus out into the hall. He speaks in a trance-like state: "That was beautifully put, Judas. Blessings on all those who know; in them the Christ lives and His glory will flow for ever and ever." Shaking himself more awake from the deep memories of the past, he continues: "You brought Golgotha here out of love for Asterius. Now tell us about your conversion as we sit around the hearth. I will light the fire."

As Jesus lights the fire, our companions enter the hall to take their proper places. Kerel sits to the left of Judas and Jesus sits on his right side. These three are the center of the group. Asterius sits next to Jesus with François at his side. Sitting at Kerel's left is Walter, with Wilfrid next to him completing a half moon. With the crescent-shaped hearth, the magic circle is formed.

In this completion something is still missing however, which is not apparent to those present. While they are seven, the three in the middle are truly one, the oneness of the Christian Ancestor, Judas Barsabas, who sits with the four companions forming the five so that both the seven and the five are represented, creating the twelve. Of the original thirteen, one is still missing and that one awaits redemption.

It is as if I am number thirteen. Am I the one to be redeemed? And who then will be my redeemer? Or is number thirteen the redeemer who will bring about the magic in my soul? I have been listening to these inner voices and my pen could not stop writing. So there they sit in the cave of my heart. Christ is now included in the twelve. What or who will be thirteen? I listen and look, and see that all are seated in their proper places. There is a quiet as if each were entering himself by watching the fire. Out of this silence, Judas' story of Golgotha wells up. Directing his words to the flames, he begins his reminiscences with difficulty and hesitation.

"I went to the Cross where Christ Jesus met with destiny. It was some weeks after the actual crucifixion and after my sickness that I dared to show openly any interest in the life of the Nazarene. I knew of Jesus and had heard about him through my emotional brother, Joseph; he was almost chosen as a disciple to replace my namesake, Judas, who had to pay with his life for his treachery. I never liked that man Iscariot and could not see why such a creature was ever elected to be one of the so-called chosen ones. If Jesus was such a great soul or man, how could he ever associate with people like that? Yet there had gathered around him many intelligent and worthwhile beings who, although perhaps not too worldly or wise, could not be led astray so easily — and I still shake my head as I attempt to comprehend how that curious group of disciples was selected.

"Now, as I think back, I feel as if the Twelve

plus Jesus were a divine unit — a band, a group of souls willing to take on and live a message, a myth. Each of them was part of the divine plan, each life being able to represent an archaic symbol in the flesh. That myth was a brutal performance of divine power, a rape of human beings obeying the New Dawn — just as the other day when you, Asterius, now, at the end of time, were so cruelly shocked by another divine power, the King of the Beasts."

Shifting in his chair and crossing his legs, he continues, rather matter-of-factly: "You know, of course, there is a great complication with a living Christ and a man like Jesus; then, also, there is my own complication over how I thought about Him while He lived and later, how I felt about Him after the crucifixion with its amazing resurrection. It is so difficult to tell you about those times, as they are now two thousand years ago. I was different, then, harder, more intellectual and slightly arrogant. Thus I could never think of Jesus as King of the Jews. I knew too many inappropriate little details of his life ever to think of him that way. I had met Him, and while one side of me was rather favorably impressed, my deep inner being must have been profoundly affected. You might say that in one way my attitude was condescending, but in another way it was very respectful. A remarkable curiosity was kindled in me after each encounter. Slight as that sometimes was, it always required a moment of meditation to figure Him out.

"You know, like so many of my friends, I was not a devout Jew. Although we learned about the teachings of Isaiah and the prophets, it was more fashionable and cultured to be conversant with the Greek philosophers and to follow the Roman civilisation. But in spite of these cultural involvements, I have a mystical side which at that time was very embarrassing to me. That irrational part of my nature relentlessly pushed me on and on and brought about a restless spirit. Moods of irony and irritation often came over me, and it was in these difficult times that I heard about the Sermon on the Mount at Capernaum. I was not there but was told about it in glowing terms by my brother, Joseph, whom I love very much. He was willing to accept a road from which I shied away. Joseph impressed me, though, and the reaction caused by Jesus' words among His listeners was formidable. Although I could not get a clear account of everything that was said, it seemed to me the people were all inspired. A flow of something, an emanation, must have come forth from Jesus which was almost too powerful for them to handle. There was a 'silent' hysteria among the crowd, which to me is a typical sign of the presence of a power greater than can be understood.

"Now that was the thing that attracted me immensely, although I never said so. This living unseen quality — this true spirit of God in a man — was what I hungered for. I did not want to go with it, but it was working in my brother and others who followed the Christ. I, by trying to undo and depreciate this quality, seemed to act like a poker stirring a fire, stimulating them still more. I secretly loved doing this, for it really proved that they were possessed by an unconquerable spirit, an inflamed psyche which, although they could not handle it intelligently, was left undaunted by my skepticism."

Judas pauses for a moment. The spell of the fire is working its way but, anxious to forestall the painful crux of his story, he tries to take his time. The inevitable reliving of the past is closing in on him, and he wonders if he will experience the accompanying agony again. He looks around at the circle in the hall, but there is no forestalling. The inner voice of memory takes over and he continues:

"My contact with Jesus was more from afar. The few times I met him, he extended just the polite, civil behavior granted to older people. I was about twenty years his senior. Jesus never tried to influence me, nor was he influenced by my social standing or riches. The fatal story of the end which all of you have preached so many times came during the Passover. Oh my God, I stayed away from it all. It made me sick with anxiety, so sick, in fact, that I could not celebrate this day of the Egyptian miracle when the blood of the Lamb was stronger than pestilence. What sign on our lintel could now again bring such salvation?

"Then I remembered an ominous dream in which I saw the red smear of blood of the Lamb form itself into a shimmering cross, which became a living, pulsating horror against a dark cloud. A star pierced this horrible vision. My soul shrieked out: 'What sacrifice and doom will come to us?' I awoke with a shock, mumbling, 'Oh, my people, my people.' My thoughts were fixed on the Babylonian exile and whether Isaiah would rise again to comfort us.

"I pushed the dream aside as being too nightmarish. The drama around me and this dream were very baffling. I possessed no insight to clarify my mind."

Judas moves around, shifts his legs and looks at his open palms; then slowly he rubs his right middle finger in a circle on his left hand, not speaking for a while. Then, talking to himself as if becoming aware for the first time, he continues:

"Unknown to myself, I was being imbued by the majesty of Christ's Being. This was the most uncanny thing of all because, looking at Him, I could see that He was very much like us. But there is in my memory of Him a magic which worked on me and everyone He met; they experienced either an uncontrollable hatred and contempt, or a deeper and deeper love toward Him and concern for their own soul.

"I took to my bed, sick and feverish from what I had heard. I was hopelessly involved in the cataclysm of the last days and, in spite of my high fever, begged everyone for information. No one could understand the reason for my anxious questioning, least of all my family. I was considered too worldly, too well balanced to show any interest in the doings of this rebellious upstart. But my spirit was in agony. I was like a house divided; the love of intellect and the love of spirit were in a deadly duel. That was the reason for my fever. The spirit penetrated and won, and I knew I had to go to the place of the supreme sacrifice: Golgotha." Then, with a deep sigh, he paused.

*The next day,
I wrote:*

So I WENT. It was a good clear day and the scene I knew so well was undisturbed. Nothing was new; nothing was different — nature lives on: the last spring flowers, the beginning of summer. The vineyards, they would do well on a day like this. All went its own way, following the endless cycle of spring, summer, fall, winter, spring, summer, fall, winter. The change was in me. The change was in me!"

It is obvious that Judas is marking time, unwilling to relive the experience of his conversion. Indeed, Judas is thinking: Will I be capable of handling that terribly gripping experience again? He looks at his companions, his travel companions in life. Will his conversion be shattered the way their churches were, their immense cathedrals, their palaces? He looks around his own Hall. Will this go, too? Jesus, sitting next to him, doesn't smile; neither does Kerel. As Jesus stares into the fire, Kerel looks toward Judas. There is anticipation, understanding and encouragement in his look. So Judas continues:

"I came to the crosses; three perpendicular beams standing like stripped trees. Only some wild flowers waving innocently in the wind were there now, my witnesses on the field of Golgotha. I knelt next to the tree in the center — denuded of branch and victim — where the great union had taken place.

"As I went deeper into prayer, the magic of the soil, the power of the Cross and the heavenly spirit united in me, and, sobbing, I fell to the ground. 'Never, never more, oh Lord, will I put my mind against Thee.' I felt the utter smallness of my being and the immensity of the Divine Spirit. I dedicated my Self, my soul, my total being to His service. Never again would I do other than follow my own path as Jesus had followed His.

"I surrendered completely to the spirit of God, and at that horrible divine moment, something tore in my flesh as if my belly, my guts were being separated from my heart. From then on, I could follow only the world of my heart. Spirit would reign supreme — and all that which belongs to flesh would have to be denied. How could that be? I would live without earth, which is God's creation also. Would I ever succeed? It was like a curse.

"For a moment, I thought: Is this a curse like that on Judas Iscariot? Have I betrayed the Lord too? But a voice in me said: 'No, dearly beloved Son of Man, this is the price to pay for your surrender. You will have to live more like a spirit than like a man in order to become the Son of God. This is the aeon of Christ, which will lead man further on his quest toward self-awareness. Your spirit will be as wine to mankind; your example will be as living bread. At all times, Spirit will have to conquer blood and flesh. Go among men, not just to teach the Gospel, but to be a man in Christ's spirit. By living in this manner you preach the Gospel. Then the Word will flow from you and you will speak as a beloved son. Through all the changes to come, there will be no change in our bondage until you and your progeny are gathered together at the end of time to unite in My house."

The prophetic inner voice of Judas of two thousand years ago has become the reality of the Now. The entire company has the same thought, the realization that they are one. They have traveled a long, hard road, alone apparently — but now they are home. They look at one another — Christ, Kerel, Judas, François, Walter, Asterius and Wilfrid. Asterius tries to fade away into his own time. Christ, aware of his neighbor's evasive mood, puts his arm gently around him and so forces him to participate in what is happening.

At that, a clap of thunder announces the nearness of the Dark Brother. With lightning speed, the whole memory of the last two thousand years passes through their minds. Their suffering, their unmarried state, their desperate efforts to withstand the denial of the flesh — all is registered with the fierce pain brought about when the essence of ourselves is touched. Their love is for a God as presented by Jesus the Christ. The hermaphroditic power in this magnificent God-man is the terrible anchor of their masculinity. This is what they faintly realized when they entered the dining hall and were greeted by the figure of Christ instead of Judas' wife.

Kerel now addresses his beloved sons: "Oh, priests of the past, what cruelty you carry. In the cosmic cycles, each aeon brings its sacrifices and its rewards. As men, your feminine spirit had to be carried by the hermaphroditic Christ. You have fulfilled your task and gathered great wisdom with the endless pain created by the spirit as the answer to all. Await now your moment of deliverance and watch him who has led you before."

Christ looks away, shaken. The time of His purity is past. Total clarity of Being penetrates Him. He knows, now, all about the tragedy of the separation, the tearing apart in the body of the two Judases — Judas Iscariot the betrayer, the one who had to live in the nether world, and Judas Barsabas, the converted, who had to live in the world of spirit. Who had suffered more, he wonders? But wouldn't both have their place of love in the eyes of God? Didn't both represent the human suffering? Didn't both fulfill their destiny? One went the way of the earth and its riches — the other the way of the spirit and the heavens.

Christ falls down on His knees. The thunder rumbles. The City of God shakes, the Beloved Son is in agony: HE PRAYS:

> "Oh, God, send greater wisdom to Me. In the mirror of time, I see the Betrayer, the Betrayed and My followers. We all play the part You assign to us, oh Lord. We are the actors who obey Your Creation. Good or bad, we obey. Lord, restore the soul of Judas who betrayed. Bless the soul of Judas who sacrificed his human nature to be Your priest.
> Lord God, recognize Your own Wholeness, gather unto Yourself all that is, all of Your Creation, to enter the New Era.
> Lord, let me die.
> For I am not worthy of Your Wholeness.
> Grant me this wish and restore the powers of Your fullness.
> Create again and anew and be aware. The world awaits Your Word.
> Give us new tongues with which to speak.

> Bless Kerel and grant him Your new Powers.
> Wholeness, o Lord! Your Humanity, Your World Soul is at stake.
> Kerel, Asterius, Wilfrid, Walter, François, Judas Barsabas,
> All in Erlo we are united.
> Grant us, oh Lord, the privilege to live our lives with grace, beauty and integrity.
> Give us the strength to carry self-awareness and bring that jewel to Your Throne."

As the Christ stands up, the Heavens release the New Music of the spheres which opens, with unseen hands, the closed doors to the Dining Hall. Bathed in a Light resplendent stands the Woman Spiritual, the Wife of God, Mother to All and Companion to the Christ, the soul of all men — the Anima Mundi!

Happily smiling and radiant, Sophia nears slowly. At the same time, unnoticed by our group, the main door of the Hall to the marketplace opens slightly, and through the crack Judas Iscariot enters. Only Christ Jesus is aware, through the tingling of his spine, that the betrayer is approaching. His Dark Brother comes closer, closer and gently, very gently, Judas enters Jesus through the backbone. This union carries the same power and feeling as an oncoming orgasm. In that final mingling of both pain and delight, they face each other. Unutterable love flows between the two as they fuse. In an explosion of Light their forces unite. So blinding is the moment that no one sees for a while. The Anima Mundi shudders in ecstasy. Her moment is here. She gives birth; She receives; She is All — She is Whole, Supreme and fully aware. Only She reigns. It is the moment of earth's magic, Spirit and Matter are one. Blindness is in the group. There is no Jesus, no Judas; instead, there is the newly born, inexperienced young man, Mr. Waterman — the divine Aquarius.

In that supreme moment of blinding Light, the Great Mother opens Her robes wide, and with an agonizing shriek which She has held back since the time of the Crucifixion, She brings forth Miriam, the beautiful bride and mate to Aquarius. Now She comes from out of the Mother, the Eternal Feminine, always there, always present but not always seen, as Her form belongs to the mystery of life.

Miriam comes toward Aquarius hesitatingly. Now that the moment is here for the encounter with the new groom, she trembles, she blushes, she senses the overpowering presence of the Great Mother. It gives her strength to go ahead, to enter life anew and differently from before. The step is great. "Will the moon still be under my feet? Will the rays of the Divine Presence still emanate as before? Will the sword still be directed toward my heart?"

All these thoughts storm her brain. Then, with a peal of laughter like crystal bells announcing the union, she shakes off all her virginal symbols. The Pietàs all over creation glow, and Christ the Son looks up at his Mother, smiles, and walks away without wounds.

Wedding bells ring. Miriam begins to speak: "Aquarius, my Lord and Mate, Servant of my Love, King of my heart, and Slave to the Divine demands of our union, here I am, like you ready for the marriage chamber. The Heavens have spoken, and as you came out of the Union of Christ and His Shadow, so I appeared through this union in Jerusalem. What a road lies ahead of us! What Heavenly or Hellish design may or will be our destiny! We will carry it together. No more will I wander alone in the Valley of Death. We will call on the Spirit Divine. We are the Spirit Divine of the Eternal Union between man and woman: female and male revealed or not revealed. We can unite at long last: we are the Union of all opposites."

Ecstatically, she falls into the arms of the astonished Aquarius; but this contact comes like an electric shock to Aquarius' body, an awakening of all that had slumbered. His potential is vitalized, his energies awaken. "Oh, my love," he says, "my love, my love, I didn't know who you were when I saw you; neither could I imagine the feelings in my heart and being caused by your presence. My God, I am home. I have a home on earth." And leaning on each other as if that would forever secure their happiness, they approach the Great Mother.

The Anima Mundi, looking at their happiness with her clear eyes, breaks out with agonizing joy: "Oh, my God, I am being pulled into human consciousness!". Fear appears in her eyes. Is she losing her divinity? No loss — she is gaining in humanity. She prays: "May my children not suffer any more in vain, but comprehend the meaning of their pain."

"Mother Goddess," speaks Aquarius, "this is my wedding gift to you. I promise that in my reign your sons and daughters will not be killed for their new ways of thought and ideals. My protection will always be there, even when the Darkness envelops them; and, as they address themselves to me, I will manifest the Light which the Christ initiated through his birth in Jesus. The suffering of your people – your children – brought me the Light of Lucifer. His Light and Christ's Light will at all times be my inseparable companions. Thus I will fulfill my dual nature."

A deep curtsy without words is the answer of the most powerful of all powers on earth, from whose womb life has started.

Miriam then speaks, looking down on her hands enfolded with those of Aquarius: "Beloved Mother, whose role I fulfilled unto the most excruciating pain of my Being, I will now go on a different road. Hard though it may be, I will not be alone, and my gift to you is that, in this happy moment, I dedicate my life, my marriage to filling the hearts of humanity with the Love I gave my firstborn an aeon ago. May our marriage be the symbol of union everywhere."

At that, a clap of thunder rolls over the mountains, here in the Engadine.

Now MY BELOVED incarnations all form a circle and dance rhythmically. They know their end is here — the end of their Piscean era. Love flows among them! They have succeeded, each in his own task. The New is born out of the Old. Nothing is lost. All has been assimilated so that the magic birth could take place. Asterius is happy as he feels the primitive and the spiritual coming together. Judas Barsabas feels the healing of his wounds. Wilfrid drops his life's burden of squabbling and trail-blazing; his job is done. Walter is freed of his guilt and is joyous. He knows that his blackness is completely redeemed. François dances, deeply contented. After the fearful journey with its sublime ending, he knows that he can have what was always deep within him, the contact with the seer. There is a fulfillment of the past which carries with it the seed and essence of the future.

We all dance together and, from their hearts, they tell me they will follow me, Erlo, the scribe, the stage, and the actor. Each slowly enters me in deep rest and contentment, and all will hopefully live harmoniously within my soul, ready to start our New Life.

Sophia, in the doorway, waits for Aquarius and Miriam, who stand in front of the fire started by the Christ. They are only half aware of what goes on. Great expectations for the aeon to come, hope in humanity, and trust in God make them happy.

Kerel prays that the marriage of Miriam and Aquarius will be fruitful for the world, and we join in fervent prayer that we may understand our newly acquired femininity, love it, cherish it and live with it until death do us part.

I, Erlo, sit in my chair next to the window in

the Waldhaus of Sils-Maria. The thunder is still in the distance. It is raining now, so there is *Tao*. My body aches; there seems to be no rest in me, although my psyche is at peace. More work is still to be done.

The last thunder has just rolled away over the mountain peaks.

SOURCES

Page 15 C. G. Jung, Memories, Dreams, Reflections. Vintage Books, New York, 1965, p. 382.
Page 24 C. G. Jung, Memories, Dreams, Reflections, p. 307.